META-CATION

Prescriptions For Some Ailing Educational Processes

Sid Jacobson

NEURO-LINGUISTIC PROGRAMMING

Meta Publications
P.O. Box 565
Cupertino, California 95014

Library of Congress Card Number 83-060320
I.S.B.N. 0-916990-11-7

Illustrations by Nancy Hakala

DEDICATION

This book is dedicated to my parents, Joe and Joanne, my brothers Steve and Dick, and my entire family for inventing me.

To Richard Bandler and John Grinder for inventing NLP.

To some very important teachers, parents, and, especially, some real special children. They're doing the best they can.

And most of all, to Judy Schuler who is so special to me. Thanks for patience above and beyond the call of sanity.

I love you all

CONTENTS

For me, after fifty years of pushing these ideas about, it has slowly become clear that muddleheadedness is not necessary.

Gregory Bateson*

*Bateson, Gregory, *Mind and Nature* (New York: E.P. Dutton, 1979), p. 209.

ACKNOWLEDGEMENTS

The author wishes to acknowledge the following people and sources, without which this volume would have been considerably less interesting, or, perhaps, not even written:

Illusions: The Adventures of a Reluctant Messiah by Richard Bach, copyright © 1977 by Creature Enterprises, Inc. Used by permission of Delacorte Press/Eleanore Friede.

Frogs Into Princes by Richard Bandler and John Grinder, copyright © 1979 by Real People Press.

Mind and Nature: A Necessary Unity by Gregory Bateson, copyright © 1979 by E.P. Dutton, Inc. Used by permission of the publisher.

NLP Vol. I by Robert Dilts, John Grinder, Richard Bandler, Leslie Cameron-Bandler, and Judith DeLozier, copyright © 1979 by Meta Publications.

Robert Dilts for permission to adapt his excellent computer programs: *Spelling Strategy* and *Math Strategy* for use in this book as well as for writing appendices II and III.

Growing Up Absurd by Paul Goodman, copyright © 1956 by Random House, Inc. (Vintage Books). Used by permission of the publisher.

The Politics of Experience & The Bird of Paradise by R.D. Laing, published by Penguin Books, Ltd. Copyright © 1967 by R.D. Laing, p. 71, reprinted by permission of Penguin Books, Ltd.

The Human Zoo by Desmond Morris, copyright © 1969, McGraw Hill Book Co. Reprinted by permission of the publisher and Jonathan Cape Ltd. on behalf of Desmond Morris.

Awareness by John O. Stevens, copyright © 1971 by Real People Press.

My warmest thanks go to Nancy Hakala for her wonderful illustrations of my cartoons.

In addition I would like to make a special acknowledgement to Richard Bandler and John Grinder for developing NLP, and therefore all of the concepts presented in this book. They are the best teachers in the world.

PUBLISHER'S NOTE

The following book by Sid Jacobson is an example of the growing fulfillment of the dream called Neuro-Linguistic Programming. As far back as 1975, there were attempts to provide teachers access to the tools of NLP; however, none of those projects reached that goal. Some became much broader publications while others were just left undone. Since that time NLP seemed to develop and change so rapidly, that books took too long to write for the NLPers to share. At last, by my request, one of us settled down to provide a book for teachers. What follows in this book represents what I hope is only the beginning for Sid. It shares NLP and does so with humor and practicality that is sorely needed in NLP literature. NLP offers choices to make your work easier, faster, and more satisfying.

Richard Bandler

INTRODUCTION: (NOT SO) RANDOM THOUGHTS

I have always been intrigued by paradoxes: the more confusing, the better. I'm sure that this has something to do with my having become a psychotherapist. Oddly enough, the most confusing paradoxes I have encountered involve the rather obscured borderline between psychology and education. The wives of two well-respected clinical psychologists—both have Ph.Ds—have asked me not to discuss learning disabilities with their spouses. Both women gave the same reasons: their husbands had been diagnosed as learning disabled when they were young. The wives felt that my "radical" views on this subject would dredge up unpleasant memories of early school years and that their husbands would become defensive.

Were the difficulties that these men faced in school because of their own disabilities or the schools'? I suspect and fear the latter; though their wives—both experienced psychotherapists—accept the former. R.D. Laing, psychiatrist and communication theorist, once pointed out the following:

A child born today in the United Kingdom stands a ten times greater chance of being admitted to a mental hospital than to a university, and about one fifth of mental hospital admissions are diagnosed schizophrenic. This can be taken as an indication that we are driving our children mad more effectively than we are genuinely edu-

1

cating them. Perhaps it is our way of educating them that is driving them mad.[1]

That's a hell of a thought.

Until I began working with school children, I took education (with the exception of my own) largely for granted: a necessary and unavoidable evil, somewhat like death and taxes. As I became more intimately involved with education, I found the analogy to be even more fitting, except that (1) Education seems more confused and less personal than either death or taxes though (2) one has a slightly better chance of overcoming its effects.

Just like health care, government, and many other "organized" human experiences, education is somewhat intangible. It should, therefore not be expected to operate as Ford's assembly line where all the cars are delivered to the end of the line in the same manner and with consistent results. Yet the assembly line is becoming the model for educating children. Why?

One reason is that we don't know, or don't ask for, what we want. If you order eggs in a diner, but fail to specify how you want them, they will probably come back scrambled. That's the fastest and easiest way.

Try to define "educated person:" A person with vast amounts of knowledge, regardless of value? Perhaps a person who is capable of integrating and organizing difficult concepts? An individual who is well rounded and has a broad perspective of the world? Someone trained to do something efficiently and effectively? I'm afraid that to most people "educated person" means a person with an education and that's all. I am convinced that—at least in the human-service professions—the number of letters following one's name means more than either the name or the knowledge gained in the letter-collection process. Whether the knowledge is useful or even relevant seems totally unimportant.

At times I have wondered if some of the assumptions at the root of our present plight in education don't have some merit.

After all, one could argue, with all of our acheivements and abilities, we *should* be able to take certain human services for granted. Couldn't we rely on the assembly-line process? Wouldn't this free us to pursue higher goals? To reach our true human potential? Well, maybe. But if so, we certainly got side-tracked somewhere along the line. We hardly seem to be heading swiftly toward our higher potentials or even effective human services. Come to think of it, maybe the assembly line never has been all it was cracked up to be (I sure wouldn't own a Pinto).

Perhaps, with all our other societal problems, it shouldn't be surprising that most of us only notice education in its grimmest moments: When a national magazine, the newspaper, or the evening news point out that a significant number of kids are graduating from high school unable to read (count, talk, think, and so forth), many of us righteously stand up and shout our most scathing indictments of the educational system in all of its non-glory. Then we forget.

Two decades ago, Paul Goodman told us: ". . . people put up with a system because 'there are no alternatives.' And when one cannot think of anything to do, soon one ceases to think at all."[2] The reverse is also true and may have come first.

At any rate, surrendering to the system is the dilemma in which we are placing much of the current generation of school children. Even if we stop blaming the system, we still will find someone and/or something to blame. That is how human beings work. Forgetting the system, we still have teachers, money, or the lack thereof, public attitudes (meaning everyone else's), social changes, the "family," and as many other favorite targets as there are people to aim at them. We have in general as much influence over those things as we have over the "system." Back to square one.

In the meantime, what happens to Johnny who can't read? He certainly has fewer choices than we do. He's stuck in a system and the system's stuck as well. We have, however, developed some extremely clever and elaborate ways to spend time and money to amuse ourselves over poor Johnny: Johnny gets screened, referred, tested, evaluated, diagnosed, and categorized until some fool finds out what *Johnny's* problem *really* is.

It is somewhat axiomatic among cynics like myself that once you begin looking for "the problem," you will certainly find it. It matters little whether it is there or not. And, it is easy to attach a very sticky label once you find "IT." Once that is done, all further difficulties can be attributed to the "disease" (deficit, syndrome, or whatever is popular that week). Besides, the label itself is often enough to give the poor kid the ailment it describes. In his book *Illusions,* Richard Bach reminds us: "Argue for your limitations, and, sure enough, they're yours."[3]

This entire process is endemic (read epidemic if you wish) among psychotherapists, educators, researchers, and others. Many insist that they are aware of the dangers inherent in labels. Then they will tell you how important it is to gather a great deal of information on each "case" in order to form a good, solid diagnosis before proceeding with treatment. That, by the way, is not a paradox. It's just plain dumb. Often, all that is ever done is further refinement of the diagnosis, ad infinitum. In some instances, treatment never begins. What is worse is that therapists and researchers teach this double-speak to educators under the guise of "expertise." The labels go everywhere. How could so many "smart" people invent such a stupid trap for themselves? It was pretty easy. Human beings are marvelously creative and flexible even in stifling their own creativity and flexibility. That isn't a paradox either. It just is.

At the heart of my highly refined cynicism (which comes and goes) is a sentiment, highly touted among cynics, that states: 90% of everything is crap. So, it is easy for me to accept the miserable state of our social institutions as inevitable. In fact, I often think the 90% figure is far too generous. In my more positive moments, however, I find the status quo not at all acceptable. But I don't want to be a guru. Just a commentator. I like the role of instigator/provoker. I love to introduce change and watch it perpetuate itself. In plain English, I think that means jump in, say my piece, jump out, and move to higher ground.

"Change" is an interesting word. Or, rather, what is interesting is its common use. Though regularly uttered by everyone, few people ever stop to think what it really means. Those who have studied the elements of change have been limited pretty much to some (but not all) systems theorists and analysts, political scientists and games theorists, logicians, communication theorists, a (painfully) few psychotherapists, epistemologists and philosophers of science, and some other not so run-of-the-mill intellectual types. Too bad. Making decisions without understanding the processes of change is somewhat like dressing in the dark. . . .

The most pervasive and useful changes always seem to be the ones that develop out of an alternative framework or viewpoint. These usually grow out of some dissatisfaction with the status quo or a major stumbling block of some sort. This is true for philosophies, theologies, sciences, societies, organizations, families, and on and on. In my circles, we call it creating alternate realities (cognitive revolutions, mental gymnastics, and other catch phrases also come to mind). But the mere thought of alternate realities is confusing for most people. When people get confused, they get scared. When they get scared, they get angry. And when they get angry in numbers, they often choose up sides for a fight: polarization, the idea that "it" has got to be "either this or that." The funny part is that "this or that" is seldom the issue. More often it is in the "either-or." How about "both," "neither," or a combination of the two?

Anthropologist Desmond Morris once wrote that the ". . . human animal is remarkably good at blinding itself to the obvious if it happens to be particularly unappealing, and it is this self-blinding process that has caused so many of the present difficulties."[4]

There seems to be an unfortunate circular truth there: Belief systems die hard, sometimes only with the believer (or not even then). When what is necessary is a new belief system, we often get stuck. And it isn't always the new system that is scary. Sometimes it is the change itself, or even just the thought of change. How do we make it so damned hard?

Attachments. Eastern philosophy has become fascinating to many people in our culture because it is so full of obvious truths. Yet that also seems to be what makes it difficult to grasp. Typically, the Zen master says to his student, "Let go, empty your mind, you don't need 'attachments' of any kind."[5] The good, American student asks for a statistical analysis that will show him the relative value of all of his attachments as well as a detailed explanation of why he should bother in the first place. He wants to formulate his next argument (that is, figure a way out of THIS one) and show the master that he is really pretty smart, too.

The master can wait. HE isn't stuck. He cracks the student on top of the head with his hand to stop the needless figuring-out process. The hardest attachments to let go of always seem to be the ones we least need, like pain and foolishness.

If we could teach our kids to painlessly switch belief systems to make their lives work, we'd all be a lot better off. On second thought, maybe they should teach us. Kids adopt alternate realities with phenomenal grace and fluidity. We call it playing (pretending). I wonder how we manage to do such a good job of teaching them to lose that important natural talent.

Wouldn't it be interesting to adopt a belief system in which learning disabilities, hyperactivity, and behavioral disorders didn't exist? The next logical step would be to get on with the task at hand: teaching kids. That would be an unusual outcome. It seems there is a woman in the inner city of Chicago who already did just that. Her ten-year-olds read and understand Dostoevsky (probably better than I do). Even the people at 60 MINUTES liked her. What a relief that was. For a while I didn't think they liked anybody. They must have thought that she was someone special. They must also have thought there was something worthwhile to be learned from her. I wonder if it was her convictions about the dignity, worth, and abilities inherent in her children?

This book is about trains of thought that result in certain belief systems. Also about certain belief systems that result in specific trains of thought. It also teaches how to avoid certain stuck belief systems. The upshot is how to help children and, just as important, how not to. Theories of development, psychopathology, traditional learning theory, and other standard fare are conspicuously absent. The reason is that much of that stuff is irrelevant. That's a pretty good reason. Besides, there is SO MUCH of that information available that the real difficulty isn't in finding it, but in avoiding it.

What follows in the first part of this book are some true stories. People who understand how human beings learn know that they learn best from stories. It's how children are taught about life at bedtime. It's how religion, morals, and other influential and important information is passed on from one generation to the next. Like most stories, the ones that follow have much in them to be found. I hope you'll grow and enjoy yourself in the search. Mostly, I let the stories speak for themselves. Occasionally I speak for them a little, hopefully in ways that enrich them. Happy exploring.

Notes

Introduction

1. R.D. Laing, *The Politics of Experience* (New York: Pantheon Books, A Division of Random House, Inc., 1967), p. 71.
2. Paul Goodman, *Growing Up Absurd* (New York: Vintage, A Division of Random House, Inc. 1956), p. xi.
3. Richard Bach, *Illusions: The Adventures of a Reluctant Messiah* (New York: Delacorte Press/Eleanore Friede, 1977), p. 75.
4. Desmond Morris, *The Human Zoo* (New York: McGraw-Hill Book Co. 1969), p. 241.
5. Part of learning Zazen, or Zen Meditation, is the practice of "emptying" one's thoughts. This is almost impossible to begin with, but even more so with intellectually oriented people. The master will often smack the student when he feels the student is too much "in his head," i.e., thinking when he should be experiencing something. It works. Almost anyone can be conditioned to do anything if you know how to interrupt the old patterns, and then replace them with new ones.

CHAPTER 1

KEEPING IT SIMPLE

Long, long ago, and far, far away, (not really but I love that beginning) I was working as a social worker in a rather traditional, family-oriented agency. Every agency has at least one or two misfits—I was about three of them. I'm a Gestalt therapist/Neuro-linguistic Programmer who dabbles in body therapy, martial arts, Eastern/Western models of integrated thought, and thinks a lot like a physicist. Got it?

Neither did many of my colleagues. Let's just say that my work was very different from traditional social work (or traditional anything).

One day a sweet little old lady (really) brought her twelve-year-old grandson in for some help. His name was Pendleton (not really). Grandma told me Pen's story. He was in special education class, and had been for six years because his I.Q. was supposedly about 50. Lately he'd been getting into a lot of fights in class. She had also noticed him fighting with other kids in the neighborhood more than usual. As she talked, I noticed that Pen was smiling. Both he and his grandma looked relaxed and at ease.

The concept of I.Q. has always triggered (and always will) the same reaction in me: I wish schools would find a more accurate measurement for placing kids—they'd probably do better using shoe size. I also found myself consciously reverting to my classical training: thinking of developmental stages, puberty, endocrinology, broken homes (he was with grandma, not ma) oedipal conflicts, and other nonsense that was still with me back in those good old days.

I told that little, nagging voice in my head to: "shut up, watch, listen, and feel or you'll miss the point." The little voice would grumble a bit, but it knew I was right. After these little internal dialogues, I would always do the same thing anyway: ask the right questions.

Me: What happens in class, Pen, when you get in fights?
Pen: They be messin' with me.
Me: Then what?
Pen: I hit 'em.
Me: Then what?
Pen: I get in trouble.
Me: But if they started it, what happens to them?
Pen: Nothin'!
Me: They don't get caught?
Pen: The teacher don't see 'em.
Me: How come?
Pen: I don't know.

I believed that, at this point, Pen really did feel like the victim and that he really wanted to talk about his predicament. I was sure I was not being conned, and my heart went out to him.

As we talked, I watched Pen's body movements. His body and his words seemed to "agree" with each other.

Bodies talk, just as words do. Usually, when people tell what they believe to be the truth their facial expressions, mannerisms, and other actions match what they are saying. Great liars can also do this but my gut reaction was that Pen was telling the truth.

As he talked, I visualized Pen in his his classroom. Visualizing people in their usual settings is important for two reasons: First, it gives me a perspective on the whole situation, not just one element, Pen. Second, it is important to design changes

that will work in an individual's environment. If I help someone to change, but that change causes more problems, I haven't done my job. A useful change should fit the person and
his or her situation. In NLP, we call this concept ecology.

I thought of other kids I had worked with who also got set
up to look stupid. Children really can be cruel to one another.
Once they find a sucker, watch out. I chuckled, cryptically,
remembering how often, as a child, the sucker had been me.
Later on, I had realized that it was just one more game to play
to fight the drudgery of compulsory education. I wished I was
flexible enough to counteract the set-ups when I was twelve
though. I'd sure have felt better about myself. Being stuck,
angry, unhappy, and predictable was really a drag. I figured
that was what Pen was feeling. I decided to keep things real
simple and to help Pen find a solution other than fighting.

> Me: Pen, can you think of anything else you could do with
> the other kids, besides hittin' 'em,[1] when they mess with
> you?
> Pen: Make friends with 'em?
> Me: (stunned) Great idea! Did anyone ever tell you that, or
> did you just think of it?
> Pen: (triumphant) I just thought of it.
> Me: Good thinkin'! It's a great idea! But do you have any
> ideas about how to do it?
> Pen: (with the wind gone from his sails) Nope.
> Me: Well let's see. . . .

I put my hand under my chin and looked a little stuck, as
Pen looked. I hadn't disagreed with anything he said. I was
startled when he suggested making friends with the other kids
though, because of the way he said it. Kids usually express
lines like that one with the enthusiasm of listening to a broken
record. In their facial expressions, they say, "If I hear 'make
friends' one more time from some adult, I shall be forced to
commit irrational acts of violence. . . ."

With Pen it was totally different. When he said that he just thought of the idea himself, he was deadly earnest. I had not experienced this before in a child and it struck me as unusual. I always look for such unusual qualities when I work with people. They're what's important.

At this point I was pretty sure that Pen would do just about anything I asked. I had already decided what I was going to try, but I wanted to motivate him while I did it. I spent the next couple of minutes pretending to painfully figure out some way to help him.

I remembered a lecture I heard in graduate school. The lecturer was one of those not so run-of-the-mill intellectual types I mentioned earlier. He was into hypnosis, brief therapy, and paradoxical interventions—essentially the art of telling someone to do something stupid, hoping that they will resist by doing something clever and productive instead. He told us what he did with children who fight in class and what he did not do with them. He told us we could do a couple of years of nondirective play therapy, talk to the parents and teachers about oedipal conflicts, or a massive variety of other garbage, depending upon our individual orientations to therapy. Then he suggested a much better idea: He would teach them to make crazy faces at the other kids rather than punch them out. I decided to try this with Pen.

Me: Pen, do you know how to make crazy faces?
Pen: Yeah.
Me: (goading) Nah, I'll bet you don't.
Pen: Yes I do!
Me: All right, let's see your best stuff.
Pen: (makes face)
Me: Not too bad, but you'll have to do a lot better than that for what I've got in mind.
Pen: What?
Me: If you can make really good faces, I'll bet you can get the other kids in trouble with the teacher.
Pen: Yeah?
Me: Sure! Cause I got an idea . . . but uh . . . (goading) nah it probably won't work, forget it.

Pen: Come on!
Me: Well, OK but we're gonna have to practice.

We, not him.

I wanted him to know that we were in this together. We both practiced making funny faces, for about five minutes. I told him which ones I liked the best for this particular project. Then I interrupted him, catching him off guard, and said: "I wonder if you could make these silly faces at kids right when they start messin' with ya." I watched Pen closely immediately after I said it. His face went blank, his eyes glazed over, I noticed his pupils dilate slightly. He appeared to be visualizing something in his head. I assumed he was imagining himself doing what I had just suggested: that he make faces at his classmates when they give him a hard time. Before he had a chance to finish the thought, or interrupt himself by saying anything, I said, "Let's practice a different way for a couple of minutes. Pretend you're in class. I'll be one of the guys giving you some trouble." I stood up and pretended to walk by him. When I was close to him, I gave him a good hard shove. In fact, I almost knocked him out of the chair. He (and grandma) stiffened up and immediately looked angry.

Me: Wait, make a face!
Pen: Oh yeah! (makes ridiculous face, laughs)

We repeated the sequence several times. I approached him from different angles. I pushed him, pinched him, and pretended to knock work from his desk. Soon his face making was just as automatic as his anger and hitting had been.

I asked him to sit back and relax. Talking very slowly and carefully, I told him what I thought would happen in class from then on. I matched the tempo of my voice to the pace of his breathing. I described the classroom: other kids, the teacher, activities, and so on. I used vague generalities, mentioning things that are standard in every classroom. I again watched him carefully. He appeared to be visualizing everything I described.

When I thought he was really experiencing the scene internally, I added what would happen the next time somebody started messin' with him. I asked him to guess just how surprised that other kid would be when he made a crazy face instead of getting angry, and how good he was going to feel that he was clever enough to outsmart the other kids like that, and what a difference it would make . . .

Then I spent a few minutes alone with grandma. I explained that all I wanted was to change the way Pen played the game in class, nothing more. I also promised her what I promise parents of almost every child I work with: "It will either work or it won't." Then I told her she would have to watch him, and listen to him, closely, to see and hear if it worked. Also, I suggested that, in a few days she ask Pen's teacher for a report.

When I saw them the next week, Pen had a big grin on his face. He said, "I made four friends this week!" Grandma told me that she had watched him closely in the playground outside their building and had seen a great difference in the way Pen handled himself with the other kids. He had not had a single fight. Both Grandma and Pen were delighted. So was I. Then Grandma said, "But if only . . ." Ah, but that is a story for yet another chapter. In the meantime, enjoy the following experiments and the next story.

Experiment #1: To Blame, Or Not

We all get stuck sometimes. We wouldn't be human otherwise. Unfortunately, we often tend to blame someone else when we are stuck. I remember consulting with a group of teachers who were complaining about one child in particular. When they were at the height of their agony, I noticed a teacher in the back of the room with a disgusted look on his face. I knew at once what was going on. After we were done, I took that teacher aside and said, "I'll bet you don't have any trouble with that kid at all." His response was, "Of course not, there is just this one, little, simple thing I noticed . . ."

Think of that one child you know that no one can handle. Then find the person who really *can*. Ask him or her how it's done. Be specific. You may really learn some easy, little approach. Then go try it! See what happens. That extra effort may really pay off.

Experiment #2: Complicated?

Teaching a child to make faces rather than fight is one of those simple, little twists that clever people have been using for years. I can not count the times I have been stuck and confused by trying to figure out some grand plan to change the course of some person, place, or thing. Then somebody came by with an obvious solution that left me feeling like an idiot. Such is life, not to mention learning.

Spend a few minutes remembering times in your life when this has happened. It's part of growing up. When you have thought of two or three examples, think of some children who could benefit from your experience. Then go, benefit them.

Once upon a time a mother brought me her ten-year-old son. Let's call him Josh. Josh's mother briefly told me that his problem was that he kept running away—from both school and home: He would just bolt out the door and be gone for hours at a time.

She knew where he went. He would go to the bus depot and hang around there. Apparently, he knew one of the drivers. Mother described this man as a big brother/father figure. He was also a friend of the family, though I never did find out what kind. There was a whole lot I never found out. Mother seemed to be playing dumb to avoid answering some of my rather pointed questions. At the time, though, I was not sure whether she was dumb or just played the role well. She also told me that Josh was retarded or at least a "slow learner." That was supposed to settle everything, I think. She wasn't clear about what she meant. But neither are those labels so I really didn't care anyway.

As she described Josh, I was watching him. He seemed detached, somehow. He was also a little fidgety—he kept looking around—but not in a way that struck me as particularly nervous. It was more exploratory: he was getting a feel for my office. Each time he saw something new (I had posters, pictures, and so forth in my office) his body would physically register the visual information. Every now and then I would interrupt his mother to ask him if what she just said was true. Fidgeting, he would nod yes, but that was all. He almost never made eye contact with me. He also never disagreed with his mother.

In these first few minutes I felt uneasy. I knew that his mother—either fully intentionally, or in part—was giving me incomplete or inaccurate information. Then she got a little more cryptic: She told me the address she had given me was for mail only. They didn't really live there. She had no telephone. If I wanted to reach her, I would have to write. I asked what to do in case of an emergency (sometimes you just have to go fishing for whatever information you can get). She told me there was an outreach worker at the project where she lived who could get a message to her. None of this stuff was *that* unusual for the clientele I was used to working with (prisons teach you a lot). But, still, I felt uneasy. There was something about the way she communicated . . .

Since Josh was not talking and his mother was being a bit hard on him, as well as generally weird, I decided to switch things up a bit. I asked her to leave so that I could spend some time alone with Josh. I was hoping that, with his mother out of the room, he would open up or at least give me some better clues.

Whenever I send parents out of my office for the foregoing reasons, I perform a little "dance." With great affect, I breathe a huge sigh of relief and say, "Whew! Now that SHE'S gone we can REALLY find out what's going on here" (I know I'm going to get letters on that one). Kids usually loosen up physically and verbally. This time my technique fell absolutely flat. Josh made it painfully and quietly clear that he was not talking. I even pulled out my "OK, I know I'm just another, dumb, white, pain-in-the-ass social worker, but c'mon, kid, give me a break . . ." routine. Nothing.

This little voice in my head would tell me all sorts of stupid things at times like this, such as, "Well, maybe he and his mother are both retarded, and this will just have to wait a few years so they can both grow out of it. . . ." Or, "He has a right to be silent. Why not play nonverbal games together for three to six months and see if he works out his oedipal problems . . ." Or, "Maybe you could give him a phobia of buses. It could be a bit of a problem later on, but at least . . ." I told the little voice to knock it off unless it could come up with something useful.

When I get really stuck, I play a little game in my head. I think of someone I know who is really clever. Then I ask myself what that person would do at a time like this. So I imagined my NLP instructor, Richard. Then I had the answer.

Richard once told a group of us that one of the reasons he learned some of the techniques he had was to avoid having to gather much verbal information. He had developed techniques whereby he could gather a minimal amount of information, and then do the rest of the talking himself. This opened up a number of avenues for me. I was pretty thoroughly trained in these techniques and tools. And I had ways of using them while, at the same time, developing a really special relationship with whomever I worked.

Establishing rapport with someone you're trying to help is a necessary and obvious first step. With someone who is verbal and willing it's easy. With Pen, for example, I just avoided arguing with him and lead him to an agreeable solution. With someone who won't talk, like Josh, the whole idea of rapport, or even agreement, gets a little cloudy, unless you have the knowledge and skills I spoke of.

I knew that if I could pace, or accurately match, some portion of Josh's ongoing experience continuously for a few minutes, I would get to a level of rapport adequate for my purposes. His whole thinking about me, and the situation, would change once he knew that I understood how he experienced himself at that moment. I know this sounds a bit sticky. To put it another way, if I could convince him that we were on a similar wavelength for at least some of the time, he would be more open to me. Hopefully, he would hear and consider whatever suggestions I came up with.

All I really wanted at that point was a chance to air my ideas about his problem and to offer alternatives. To pace some portion of his experience was really a pretty easy task. I simply decided to "feed back" to him whatever he was overtly doing with his body (This technique is called biofeedback.) But I wanted to do it in a way that would gain and hold his attention. So I started with a story.

"Josh, you remind me of another kid, just about your age, I saw not too long ago. In fact, he looked a lot like you. And you know what? This kid was really CRAZY! I wonder if you are too."

At this point Josh lit up like a Christmas tree. He looked really startled, then confused. That's what I wanted. Confusion is a very useful tool in general, but especially at times like this. I sure as hell had his attention. Pretending to talk about this "other" kid, I just started to comment on what he was doing. I also matched the pace of my voice with the rise and fall of his chest as he breathed in and out.

"Yeah, Josh, that crazy kid sat in *that very chair* where you're sitting now. And he would look up at the ceiling (as Josh looked up at the ceiling), then look down (as Josh looked down), then slide back in his chair (as Josh did)," and so forth.

After about five minutes of this, Josh was showing the signs I was looking for. His body had become a little rigid, but relaxed, his pupils were slightly dilated, and his movements looked as if he had gone onto "automatic pilot."

I wanted to know if I had paced his experience well enough to lead him to new ones. I tried suggesting something to find out if I had.

"And, Josh, as that kid looked up (as Josh did), and wiggled his feet, (as Josh did), he found himself getting *very very tired.*"

When I said that Josh's shoulders slumped slightly, his eyes half closed, and he yawned. I figured I was on the right track, so I continued. I kept commenting on what he was doing, within the story, and interspersed what he was doing with comments about how tired that other kid had gotten. It seemed to work better as I continued. I decided it was time for the really important suggestions.

"And, Josh, you know what I found out about that other kid? He wasn't crazy after all! He had just made some mistakes he had to fix. Like stayin' where he was s'posed to. Yep, he found out he would *feel a lot better, Josh,* when he stayed with his momma and stayed in class. And he got a lot happier, too."

For several minutes I repeated this part of the story, and embellished it. After I had told it in several different ways, I stopped. The entire process had taken about twenty to twenty-five minutes.

"Josh, that was some story, huh? Well I know you're still real tired, so I'm gonna let you go home with your momma in a couple of minutes. And, by the way, as you walk out the door of my office, you'll be wide awake."

I opened the door for him. As soon as he passed through the door he stopped suddenly in the middle of the hallway. He looked around, a bit frantically, as if he were lost. I led him back to where his mother was waiting. He looked confused but not upset.

I spent a few minutes talking with his mother. I observed her closely as we talked, because I again had those feelings of something being very wrong. I still didn't know what, though. We scheduled another appointment, and she left.

I saw her and Josh about three or four weeks after that initial session. Josh had run away twice: once from school and once from his mother, the day after I had seen them. Then he stopped completely. He hadn't run away for almost a month, whereas it had been an almost daily ritual before. Mother said he was OK now, and she didn't want to come back. I told her I wanted to stay in touch, though. I still felt funny about the whole thing. And I had come up with some really nasty hunches shortly after the first session.

Whenever a child is into running away, there is a reason. It isn't just a bad habit. It can be treated that way, which is essentially what I had done. But I knew it was only a start. The only reason I had treated it that way at all was that I didn't see many other choices at the time. I knew that if the running stopped, which it had, the reasons for it would soon show themselves in some other way. Sooner or later I would have to get reinvolved. That's why I wanted to stay in touch.

This was one of those uncomfortable times when there is nothing else to do but wait a while. For an action-oriented guy like me, it was almost torture. But that goes with the territory. It was especially hard because of my scary suspicions. But we need to set this story aside for a while and go on to other things. While you wait patiently for the continuation of this story, do the following experiment.

Experiment #3: As If . . . [2]

Have you ever found yourself enjoying someone for their talents? (If not, see a doctor!) There are many people who can make the hardest things look effortless. We wonder how they do it. Then we pass it off to brilliance, genetics, hormones, or luck. But we don't have to.

Think of someone with a special talent for communicating with children. Pretend for a few minutes that *you are that person*. Stand or walk the way that person does. Steal their posture, carriage, voice, thoughts. Now think of some problem you are having with a child. Imagine what you would do *as that talented special person*. How would you see or hear this child? How would you feel about the child as this other person? When you think you have the idea, approach that child *as if you were* that other person. See what happens.

Notes

Chapter 1

1. Imitating diction is one technique used in pacing.
2. This experiment is based on "The *As If Frame,*" a concept introduced to NLP by John Grinder, one of the co-founders of NLP. Presented in numerous workshops.

CHAPTER 2

WEIGHING ANCHORS

It came to pass that a friend of mine got a part-time job, working with an autistic child. She was babysitter, companion, big sister, and tutor to this little girl. She told me about it one evening after a class we were taking together. She asked if I knew anything about autism and if I had any advice. I said, "Yes and yes." Then I asked her what, exactly, she wanted to accomplish with this little girl.

She said the little girl could do some things, some times. The girl was in a special school program and had some work to do that my friend wanted to help her with. She figured that would be a good start. She also told me that she knew people did all sorts of fancy behavior modification with autistic children and that it sometimes worked. I responded that that was especially true with errorless learning paradigms[1] (she looked at me as if I were speaking Martian). I also added that, even though it was often successful work, it was extremely tedious. My friend admitted having little experience with this type of behavioral work, other than having read about it. She was a little hesitant, but willing.

I asked her if she knew about "anchoring." She said, "No." I told her that it was an NLP way of talking about classical (Pavlov's) conditioning, but it made a lot more sense. She said she knew about "pairing," or conditioning one thing to another, but she wasn't sure what to connect with what (why, when, or how). I told her that it was a lot easier to do than she thought. She could establish a signal (an "anchor") that would immediately bring the little girl to a mood (or state of consciousness/awareness) in which she was able to perform at her level best. It was a way of bringing all the little girl's internal resources, strengths, and abilities to bear. I told her we call this a resource anchor. My friend was highly skeptical. I proposed that she try the following experiment.

I asked her to pick a time and place in which the little girl was doing something really well *and* enjoying herself. She replied that, each afternoon, she sits with the child and does homework (of a sort). Sometimes the little girl would do fine and enjoy herself. But, at the slightest sign of difficulty or pressure, she would blow up and throw a semivolcanic tantrum. So far my friend had been unable to find or establish any consistent pattern. As a result, homework, and almost everything else, was a totally hit-or-miss proposition. I responded that her description was typical of children described as autistic. That was the reason that errorless learning, in effect guiding all behavior to correct responses, was developed. Frustration never occurs. But, if she did what I told her, she could take the whole idea a quantum leap farther.

I told her that, the next time the little girl was in that initial efficient and enjoyable state of mind, she should reach around her and calmly and naturally place her hand on the girl's shoulder. She was to pay special attention to the exact location and pressure of the touch, so that she could duplicate it, precisely, at will.

I explained that this touch would become a part of the little girl's internal experience of herself while she was in that positive state of mind. And it would be most effective if she repeated it when they sat in the same room doing the same task: homework. If she used this technique properly the little girl should be able to maintain that same positive mood. Hopefully, this would lead to the consistency she had been lacking. I suggested that the term consistency should be used only to describe the little girl's state of mind and abilities. None of this vague reward-and-punishment, robotic thinking. That would lead her astray. My friend agreed, albeit with great skepticism, to try the experiment.

I saw her a week later. She reported the following:

> I did exactly what you said. Each day we sat down in the same place in the room and I put my hand on her shoulder, like you said. She seemed fine each day, but I figured she was just feeling good that week. So the fifth day, I just sat down next to her and did nothing. I had already decided you were crazy for devising an experiment like this, anyway, and I was going to prove it. But as I sat there, nothing happened. The little girl sat there doing nothing at all. It was like she was waiting for something to happen. She gave me a couple of strange looks. After a couple of minutes of this she reached over, picked up my hand, and put it on her own shoulder, just as I had been doing. Then she smiled, sighed, and started her work. I COULDN'T BELIEVE IT.

I could.

Experiment #4: Do You Believe . . .

Reality is a tough concept. Truth is even worse. Both are incredibly elusive and totally dependent on your frame of reference besides. Isn't it strange that most of our arguments with one another really come down to, who is right? What an incredible waste of time and energy! And what a useless way to hurt each other's feelings.

Just fifty years ago, the idiom in the English language to describe the ridiculously impossible was: "Why, that's as crazy as trying to put a man on the moon!"[2] Funny how the impossible becomes the mundane in a few short years. Expecially in all the fields of technology. But isn't education a set of technologies? Spend some time thinking about things that you were absolutely sure were impossible. But they happened anyway. Do any of them involve school children? If not, think harder.

I once had an adult client with whom I was doing essentially nothing-on a monthly basis. His name was Russ. The reason we had undertaken this Herculean task was that there was nothing else we wanted to do. Social workers sometimes have clients assigned to them by the courts or some related institution just to "keep an eye on" them. Russ was one such client. Such is life in the legal/medical/social systems we live in.

After some time, though, Russ confided in me that there was something in his life that bothered him. He could barely read. This surprised me. His verbal ability and his memory for auditory detail were remarkable. He could recite whole portions of comedy albums (one of my favorite pastimes as well). As he had with his previous worker, we had been sharing stories for months. It really is a fine way to pass the time when you have nothing else to pass. After he told me about his reading problem, we had the following conversation:

Me: What happens when you read?
Ru: I just can't.
Me: Not at all?
Ru: Well no. I can read a little. I can get through a few things in the newspaper. And they gave me a test once on reading. They said I read about like a second grader.
Me: So you can read some. What happens when you do?
Ru: I get mixed up. I mess up a lot of words.

I then pointed to a poster on the wall and said, "Read that for me." Russ craned his neck, stiffened up, held his breath, squinted his eyes, and (after some coaxing) plunged ahead. He did all right on the shorter words. On the longer ones, he tended to reverse parts of the words. If the word was more than three or four syllables long, he would transpose the last couple of syllables, delete one and reverse another, or some other combination of deletion and reversal. The most notable thing, however, was that he was frustrated, tense, and worn out after about five minutes. And pretty disgusted with himself.

I told him to relax for a couple of minutes. I taught him how to breathe properly and deeply by directing his breath to the lowest part of his abdomen first and then to fill up his chest.

I told him to shake out the tension in his neck and shoulders by wiggling his hands and arms and rolling his head around in slow circles. Then I told him to sit quietly for a few moments. He felt much better.

I then asked him to try again, very slowly, but only to go as fast as he could and still feel comfortable. He immediately did much better. Once I told him what the longer words *sounded* like, he was much more comfortable with them. While he was doing this, I spoke to him in a slow, relaxed, and care-free voice. And the tone of my voice was lower and "softer" in feeling as well as volume. I wanted the calm tone of my voice to become an anchor for his calm feelings. So I asked him— always speaking in the same, calm tone—to do a few more things. As I did so, he remained calm and relaxed.

I suggested that, from now on, he could do this on his own. Each time he picked up something to read, or learn, he could first relax, then notice how much easier the material seemed. He said that his wife had been helping him with his reading for years and that he was sure what I taught him would help. He also said that, in the future, he would pay much closer attention to his feelings.

At this point, I flashed back in my mind to some of the training I had had. I thought to myself about the importance of that last step he and I had done together, called future-pacing, in NLP language.

I had learned that many therapists and teachers are very adept at getting someone to be able to do something in the office or classroom. But the person doesn't seem to take what they've learned home. This makes perfect sense when you stop to think about it. Many moods (states of consciousness/awareness) are tied or anchored to a particular setting. Even though Russ could be relaxed with me in my office, he would not necessarily have the same experience at home with his wife, or at work with his boss. Different places (and people) don't look, sound, feel, or smell the same by any means. (That's one of the major reasons that I spend more of my time in Italian restaurants than in sewage-treatment plants.) Most important, psychologists have known for a long time that many things learned and/or experienced in one particular state of consciousness are much better remembered in that same state.[3]

From that point on, each time Russ would read he would pay closer attention to his feelings and get nice and relaxed. In effect, he would go back to the same state he was in at my office, as much as possible. He was a capable and well-motivated adult who could, and would, learn rapidly with the proper instruction. It's really that way most of the time.

I used a similar—but more complex—process with little Pen. I wanted him to enjoy school and feel good in class. This usually isn't too hard as long as there isn't some good reason for a kid to be uncomfortable. As I said earlier, getting Pen to make faces and relax at the right time simply took a little role playing, as practice. Future pacing required another step called guided fantasy.

A guided fantasy is simply an imagined experience containing sights, sounds, feelings, smells, and tastes (when appropriate). The guide structures it so that anyone having the fantasy will learn something useful. Pen got my standard classroom trip.

I began with a relaxation exercise developed especially for children. It's called the dreaming arm technique. I asked Pen what his favorite TV show was. He said, "Abbott and Costello." Then I asked him if he knew about his dreaming arm. He, of course, looked puzzled and said no. First, I gave him a hard time about it to raise his level of curiosity. Then I told him. I said that if he lifted his left arm in the air just right, he would be able to remember his favorite episode of Abbott and Costello. Then he could let his arm drift down slowly to the arm of his chair, but only as quickly as he watched the whole show in his mind's eye. And I added the suggestion that, by the time he had finished watching the show, his eyes would be closed and he would feel deeply relaxed.

Then I told him to listen to me while I told him what I wanted him to see and hear next. I asked him to make a picture of his classroom in his head. He was to see, clearly, the teacher, the other kids, desks, chairs, blackboard, and so forth. I guided him from object to object, slowly over the next several minutes. I repeatedly suggested that he *see how good he was feeling,* as he looked around. This was sort of a rigged game since he was already feeling really good and relaxed. I had set up the dreaming arm as a permanent anchor to make him feel good whenever we did it. Now the internal pictures of his classroom became anchors for the same set of internal experiences. In essence, whenever he thought of his class, he should feel the same way he did during the fantasy: good and comfortable.

Then I continued to guide him through his classroom, noting sounds. I told him to pay attention to the rustle of papers, scratching of pencils, movement of chairs, chalk on the board, the teacher's voice, other kids' voices as well as his own, and so forth. Again, interspersed with these were reminders of how good he was feeling.

I repeated this exercise again, emphasizing special feelings associated with the classroom. I asked him to notice if he could feel the wooden chair and desk, the pencil in his hand, the temperature (I threw in the smell as well) of the air, and so forth. Again, all of this portrayed against the background of his good feelings.

The entire fantasy took about fifteen to twenty minutes. The structure, again, was to create new anchors. These were all objects, sounds, and feelings found in the classroom. They were the sum of things that made up the "atmosphere" of his class. Provided that he was really relaxed and comfortable while I took him through the fantasy, he should feel that way in the classroom as well.

The obvious question was, how could you ever know for sure that he would go into that same exact state of mind when he went to class. The obvious answer is that you can never know for sure. Ideally, he would go in feeling and experiencing his classroom with at least some of the positives I had suggested. Would he be exactly the same as in the office? No. He would probably develop a state of mind with most of the features of that fantasy, but because the fantasy couldn't possibly be *the same as* the classroom, his state of mind wouldn't be exactly the same either. What he would have would be an experience unique to him, a unique human being. And experience tells those of us who do this kind of work that it would be uniquely useful to him as a person.

Experiment #5: Experiencing the Obvious[4]

When is the last time you were in a school classroom? Even if it is recent, did you try it from a child's point of view? Go, sit alone in a classroom somewhere, at a student's desk. Look around. Let your eyes wander and see what attracts, or distracts, your attention. Listen to your own internal dialogue for a few moments. What are you telling yourself? What memories come back? Are they fond memories or . . . ? What do you feel as you look around? Most obvious to me about this experiment is that everyone will have their own ideas about what is obvious . . .

Notes

Chapter 2

1. An errorless learning paradigm, as the name implies, is a structure or procedure for working with a person that forces or guides the person to the correct answers all the time. A good example is in teaching a child to put round pegs in round holes on a board. Each time the child would try to place the peg into a hole that was square or into which the peg would not fit, you would push his or her hand over to the correct hole, avoiding the possibility of error. This is effective with so-called autistic children because they generally can't stand to make errors. It avoids frustration, creates constant positive reinforcement, but is extremely tedious.
2. Richard Bandler, "Fabric of Reality," (Paper presented at second annual NLP conference, 1981).
3. This principle is called state-dependent learning or state-specific learning. It is the key to understanding why people cannot remember what they did or what happened to them while they were drunk or under the influence of a drug. These memories are not really lost. To recall them, one must take the same drug or drink, in other words, re-enter that same state of consciousness. This principle is also the basis for the phenomenon known as post-hypnotic suggestion.
4. This is a standard Gestalt-Therapy experiment.

CHAPTER 3

THE EYES HAVE IT

Come back now to a time when Pen and his grandmother and I left off (Chapter 2). We were all delighted with Pen's progress in making friends and avoiding fights. He had seemingly licked those problems. Then she and I had the following conversation:

Gr: But if only he could learn. If only somebody could teach him.

Me: What do you mean? What can't he learn? Can he read (most impatiently)?

Gr: READ?! He can't even say the alphabet (sadly).

Me: (under my breath "Oh x@!!") How long has he been in special education?

Gr: This is his seventh year.

Me: They did a terrific job (even more disgusted than the words would indicate).

Actually, my head was swimming at this point. I was so angry and disgusted with a system that had failed so miserably that I almost wanted to cry. I was also bound and determined to do whatever repair work was necessary. Pen was going to get something out of school besides frustration. I figured that since he was feeling better in class, and making friends, now was the best time to help him. I also knew that, with my NLP skills, I could teach rings around just about any teacher in any school.

I began, as always, by finding out exactly what Pen did when attempting to recite the alphabet. In NLP, we call this process "strategy elicitation." That's a fancy way of saying, "finding out what he does." I then said the magic words, "Pen, say the alphabet for me."

Pen looked almost straight up, and slightly to his left. He then began to recite, in a dull, slow monotone, "A,B,C,D," and so forth. When he got to the sequence L,M,N,O,P he faltered and stopped. He was unable to continue, so I watched closely as he went back to the beginning. His eyes and head actually shifted back to the left, then he started again. His repetition was in the same tone, and he faltered in the same spot. He tried a third time—it was identical to the first two. He failed at L,M,N,O,P. Each time his eyes and head went through the same movements. Each time his voice echoed the same dull, slow monotone. I glanced over at grandma who said, "It's always the same. And it's funny, his sister sings it right off."

It was clear to me that I had more than enough information to help Pen. First of all, Pen had the alphabet arranged as a picture in his head, from left to right. I knew this, because his eyes shifted up and to his left. For most people, eye movement in the direction of up and to their left indicates that they are visualizing a memory, whether they are aware of it or not. The following section, taken from *Neuro Linguistic Programming: Vol. I,* will give you an adequate summary of eye-movement patterns that are useful in this process.

3.231 Eye Movements as Accessing Cues

We have noticed that the eye movements people make as they are thinking and processing information provide a remarkably accurate index for sensory specific neurological activity. We introduced these patterns in *Patterns II:*

"When each of us selects the words we use to communicate to one another verbally, we typically select those words at the unconscious level of functioning. These words, then, indicate which portions of the world of internally and externally available experience we have access to at that moment in time. More specifically, the set of words known as predicates (verbs, adjectives and adverbs) are particularly indicative. Secondly, each of us has developed particular body movements which indicate to the astute observer which representational system we are using. Especially rich in significance are the eye scanning patterns which we have developed. Thus, for the student of hypnosis, predicates in the verbal system and eye scanning patterns in the nonverbal system offer quick and powerful ways of determining which of the potential meaning making resources—the representational systems—the client is using at a moment in time, and therefore how to respond creatively to the client. Consider, for example, how many times you have asked someone a question and they have paused, said "Hmmmmm, let's see" and accompanying this verbalization they move their eyes up and to the left. Movement of the eyes up and to the left stimulates (in right handed people) eidetic images located in the non-dominant hemisphere. The neurological pathways that come from the left side of both eyes (left visual fields) are represented in the right cerebral hemisphere (non-dominant). The eye scanning movement up and to the left is a common way people use to stimulate that hemisphere as a method for accessing visual memory. Eye movements up and to the right conversely stimulate the left cerebral hemisphere and constructed images—that is, visual representations of things that the person has never seen before (see *Patterns,* volume I, page 182).

"Developing your skill in detecting the client's most highly valued representational system will give you access to an extremely powerful utilization tool for effective hypnotic communication. There are two principal ways which we have found effective in teaching people in our training seminars to refine their ability to detect representational systems:

(1) attending to accessing cues which may be detected visually. Specifically (for the right-handed person):

accessing cue	representational system indicated	
eyes up and to the left . . .	eidetic imagery	(V)
eyes up and to the right . . .	constructed imagery	(V)
eyes defocused in position . . .	imagery	(V)
eyes down and to the left . . .	internal dialogue	(A)
telephone positions . . .	internal dialogue	(A)
eyes left or right, same level of gaze . . .	internal auditory	(A)
eyes down and to the right . . .	body sensations	(K)
hand[s] touching on midline . . .	body sensations	(K)

I knew Pen well enough to know that he fit this scheme perfectly. It only takes a couple of minutes to determine this, anyway. You just have to ask the right questions, as always.

Also, it was clear that he was "reading" his picture from left to right, because I could see his eyes (and head) scanning that way. I was also pretty sure that he had almost no corresponding awareness of the sounds of the letters, or even his voice, as he recited. The monotone he recited the alphabet in was very different from his normal speaking voice. I knew that, normally, this strategy should be adequate for reciting the alphabet. But for some reason it didn't work for Pen.

Next, I wanted to verify all of my ideas. So I asked Pen if he was actually seeing the alphabet in his head. He said he was. I also asked him if he was having some kind of trouble with the picture when he got to *L,M,N,O,P.* He said yes, again.

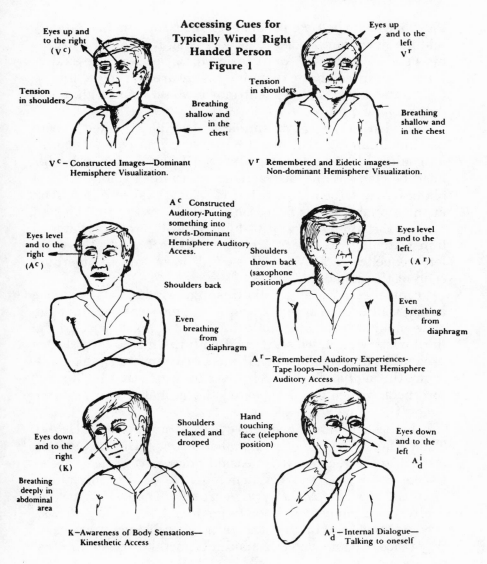

Accessing Cues for Typically Wired Right Handed Person
Figure 1

Eyes up and to the right (V^c)

Tension in shoulders

Breathing shallow and in the chest

V^c – Constructed Images—Dominant Hemisphere Visualization.

Eyes up and to the left V^r

Tension in shoulders

Breathing shallow and in the chest

V^r Remembered and Eidetic images—Non-dominant Hemisphere Visualization.

A^c Constructed Auditory-Putting something into words-Dominant Hemisphere Auditory Access.

Eyes level and to the right (A^c)

Shoulders back

Even breathing from diaphragm

Shoulders thrown back (saxophone position)

Eyes level and to the left. (A^r)

Even breathing from diaphragm

A^r – Remembered Auditory Experiences-Tape loops—Non-dominant Hemisphere Auditory Access

Eyes down and to the right (K)

Breathing deeply in abdominal area

Shoulders relaxed and drooped

Hand touching face (telephone position)

Eyes down and to the left A^i_d

K – Awareness of Body Sensations—Kinesthetic Access

A^i_d – Internal Dialogue—Talking to oneself

I asked if he became uncomfortable when the picture got scrambled. He said, and his body showed me, absolutely yes.

I then thought for a moment about why this strategy could possibly be ineffective here. I decided that I really didn't care;

I just needed to help Pen change it. And Grandma had already told me how. Pen needed to either, "sing it right off," just as his sister or at least *hear* it inside his head while he said it. I was convinced that expanding his awareness by adding in the "soundtrack" to his silent movie would be enough. I still didn't know quite why.

I decided to keep it as simple as possible. I asked Pen to use his dreaming arm to get as relaxed and comfortable as he could. When he felt comfortable, I asked him to let his head be clear of any distractions. (Actually I said, "Make a blank movie screen in your head.") Then I asked him to look at the alphabet in his head "only as I sing it to you." I began to sing the alphabet song to him while I carefully watched him watching his internal picture. When I got to the problem sequence, *L,M,N,O,P,* I slowed down and exaggerated each of the sounds.

I continued normally. I did this to mark out that sequence as one that needed special attention.[1] I also wanted him to go slow enough to remain comfortable and relaxed, even in the hard parts. Again, we started off with the method we always used to get him comfortable. It was also connected to his classroom, through anchoring. This was to insure that he "took it to school with him." I repeated the alphabet two or three times, the same way each time.

I then asked him to open his eyes and stay relaxed. He did. Then I said, "Pen, say the alphabet for me." He started with a much more relaxed and pleasant voice, sort of halfway between my singing and his monotone. He comfortably glided right through *L,M,N,O,P* with no trouble. Then a strange (not really) thing happened. When he got to *S,* he said, *"X,"* floundered, got lost, and had to start over. He repeated it the same way twice. He knew he was making a mistake, but he was just as stuck as before.

By this point, he had reversed his strategy to a totally auditory one. *S* and *X* sound almost the same, though they look quite different. I asked Pen if he could see that part of the alphabet in his head. He said it was hard. I remembered that he could recite the first half of the alphabet fine all along, but he hadn't gotten this far before. At least not with me, and not enough to have formed a good internal picture of it.

I wrote out the alphabet on a small piece of paper. I asked Pen to do the dreaming-arm technique again. I told him we were going to do it the same way, except that, this time, I wanted him to look at *my* picture of the alphabet, which I had drawn on a piece of paper. I sang it again, two or three times, and pointed to *S* and *X,* when I got to them. (This emphasized these two letters separately from the rest.)

I then asked him to take a breath and recite the alphabet. He did so perfectly three times in a row. It was the first time in his life. The three of us were rather ecstatic.

Next, I did more of the future pacing that I talked about earlier. I took him through another guided fantasy of his classroom. This time, however, I added important suggestions. I told him that since he now knew the alphabet, it would be much easier for him to learn to read: it would be comfortable, and he would really enjoy it. From that point on, he was going to begin to learn important and fun things. All this was going to make him a more interesting, better, and happier person: one both he and his grandmother could be proud of. And it was all because he worked so hard in a really fun and relaxed way.

I always add suggestions like those to all the work I do with people. I think it is important to do more than just solve problems—though that is certainly worthwhile. These suggestions put problems into a framework of growth and personhood. I organize the suggestions so that each hurdle that is overcome becomes a building block for future growth as well as a solved problem: each solved problem becomes a blueprint for future solutions. (This is certainly my personal value judgement. I keep it because I think it is a worthwhile one to have.)

Another value of mine is to intellectually understand what I do as thoroughly as possible. As I said earlier, it was not necessary for me to know exactly *why* Pen had the particular trouble that he did. I knew I could help him regardless. The whole process only took about forty-five minutes and was effective. This was, in part, because I didn't bother to try to figure it all out. But I am in the business of packaging and teaching strategies that are effective for other people. So I wanted to know. Especially since I had considered Pen's visual representation of the alphabet to be a perfectly good one. Shortly after I finished this piece of work, I spent a few quiet minutes reflecting on the whole set of processes involved here. A better way of putting it might be to say that I was "playing detective." Then it hit me.

In the sequence *L,M,N,O,P,* there is a built-in problem for someone with *only* a visual image of the letters. That is, *M* and *N* look very similar. When someone sees two similar things, their natural tendency is to glance quickly back and forth between them to distinguish between the two. This is a fine way to make subtle distinctions, but it is a really lousy strategy for completing a sequence.

In effect, to complete the sequence *L,M,N,O,P,* you need to visualize the letters in that order. One letter acts as a cue for the next. If you ask people where a particular letter falls in the alphabet, many adults will have to start from the beginning to be able to answer you correctly. This indicates that they have it arranged in order in their minds.

Pen's visual strategy must have been something like this:

$$J \rightarrow K \rightarrow L \rightarrow M \underset{\longrightarrow}{\overset{\longleftarrow}{}} N$$

The loop between *M* and *N* must have just continued without the proper distinction ever being made. This loop never did cue the subsequent letters of the alphabet. His frustration grew each time this happened until it appeared overwhelming.

A more complete description is: he started with a set of visual images; at the problem sequence, it became difficult to keep the picture clear; he had physical discomfort at this point; the bad feelings became more powerful, that is he was more aware of them than of the visual representation; he could then no longer *see* while he paid attention to how bad he *felt;* the more the picture scrambled, the worse he felt; the task at hand became less important than feeling miserable; he would give up. He really didn't have a choice by the time he felt that way. But, he was still sitting in front of someone who was waiting to hear him say the alphabet. I was convinced that he would try to please that someone until he got exhausted. He would start over and fail at the same point as long as there was someone he wanted to please. Even though he knew he was doing something that didn't work, he didn't have anything else to replace it with.

All of this may sound too complicated. It is. Remember these were just my (not so) random thoughts at the time. And, admittedly, not many people think the way I do, randomly or otherwise. It isn't necessary. The only thing that is necessary is the ability to help someone change something that doesn't work to something that does. Indeed, I didn't consciously think, step by step, of all I just described. Mainly, I was concerned with Pen's visualization at a particular sequence, his lack of auditory awareness, and his discomfort. The other stuff was for my enlightenment.

I once had an experience in a workshop that illustrates how to use visualization. My former partner and I were making a presentation at a school for teachers and parents. As in most introductory NLP demonstrations, we wanted to give them an example of a strategy that works for spelling. We asked for some good spellers in the room to volunteer themselves. We asked the volunteers to spell a couple of words for us. We asked the rest of the group to watch closely. Each one—as do all good spellers—did exactly the same thing: they looked up and to their left, and then spelled the words correctly. By asking them the appropriate questions, we made it clear to everyone present that, as these people looked up and to the left, they were visualizing the word. Then they "read" it to us. They knew they were correct by a feeling they had. (Some people check themselves by the sound of the word rather than the feeling, but almost all good spellers do one or the other.) They all said they knew whether they had it right because it *felt* right or did not. They said they rarely made mistakes.

We then asked if there were any really bad spellers in the

room. The teachers all began to laugh and point at Steve, the physical education teacher. They said he was the worst speller around. Several remarks were passed attesting to his good fortune at getting his own name right the majority of the time. They also said how much fun it was to torment him unmercifully. Especially since he was so capable in many other areas.

When the jokes died down, we asked Steve to spell a couple of words for us. Each time he would look down and to the right, then to the left, back and forth, and everywhere but up. He became tense and really uncomfortable and was, essentially, unable to spell.

We asked him to take a couple of deep breaths and to relax for a moment. When he felt better, we asked him a couple of questions about how he had managed to get this far in life, as well as in education, without being able to spell. He told us he always had a dictionary nearby. He never hesitated to use it.

My colleague and I looked at each other for about one fourth of a second. Then we explained in detail what we knew about visualization. We told the group that, essentially, we all have photographic memory (technically known as eidetic imagery). In fact our memories are remarkably complete. Many people, including me, choose to believe that everything we have ever experienced, that is, seen, heard, felt, tasted, or smelled, is stored intact in our brains.[2] We automatically store information that comes in through our senses. Effective "retrieval," on the other hand, has to be taught and learned. Understanding more about *how* retrieval works, in experiential terms, can improve us tremendously.

Understanding eye-movement patterns is important. Since most people look up and to their left to retrieve visual-stored information, it stands to reason that it is a natural phenomenon of some sort (even without the supporting neurological evidence). We assumed that Steve, after years of exposure to the dictionary, probably had most of it stored. He just didn't have a way of getting to that stored memory.

My colleague went over to Steve and helped him relax by doing a quick exercise. Then she asked him to spell some words. He was to visualize the dictionary. He was then to imagine opening it, turning the pages while simultaneously watching the guide words at the top of each page, finding the page with the word on it, looking down the page to find the word, then reading us the word. For the first word he took a breath and began looking around as before. We both said, "No, up and left, with your eyes." He looked up and began again. His face brightened. I said, "Now look carefully at the guide words, then look down the page." He said, "I don't have to. It is the guide word." He then spelled it smoothly, easily, and correctly, just by reading his own internal dictionary. When he finished the word, he immediately looked forward, wide-eyed, as if stunned and said, "I'll be damned." We practiced a couple more words until everyone in the room was convinced (especially Steve) that he had almost the entire dictionary at his disposal. He simply had to look in the right place.

We were using much the same strategy and technique that I used with Pen. Relaxation was important, as always. So was the ability to visualize. So was the fact that we used a major strategy already being employed by Steve, and changed it slightly. With Pen, I kept his visualization pretty much intact and added the auditory component. With Steve, we took his external use of the dictionary and "internalized" it. That is we made it faster, easier, less traumatic, and more graceful. Most people have what they need to function, whether they are "retarded" children or competent adults. Sometimes the more subtle approaches are the best.

Experiment #6: How Are You Organized?

You have probably just learned about the importance of eye-movement patterns for the first time. Within the basic pattern, there are a few characteristics that are different in different individuals. For example, some people, myself included, can visualize, regardless of the direction of gaze and equally well with eyes opened or closed. Others can't. It may be interesting to find out more about how you, internally, are organized.

Start by visualizing something, perhaps a difficult word to spell. Where is the picture the clearest? Straight ahead? Up and to the left or to the right?

Once you have established the easiest way for you to visualize, find out if there is a direction of gaze that makes visualizing difficult or impossible. For many people, making an internal picture while looking down is impossible. Find out whether this is true for yourself.

Repeat the above instructions, for sound and feelings. Listen to a tune in your head while looking down and to the left. See if that is the way that you "hear" it most clearly. Then try hearing it while looking in another direction, say up and to the right. Next, pay attention to your feelings. (Probably, this will be easiest if you move your eyes down and to the right, or straight down.) Find out.

The chart and explanation (on page 41) should help you devise some more interesting combinations to explore. Have fun with it!

Once in a while, you run into someone who is doing something in a way that, fundamentally, won't work very well. One example is Russ, who could barely read. Once we worked on his ability to *see* the words (inside as well as out) and relax while reading, there was still more to do. He told me, just as Steve had, that he couldn't spell. He was convinced that, if he could learn to spell, everything else would fall right into place. He said so with such conviction that I believed him. I didn't think that understanding why this was true was particularly relevant to the task at hand. So I didn't bother to try. I felt that believing along with him would suffice.

I asked him how he spelled. He said if he could not sound out a word, he didn't bother to try at all. He also said that some teacher he had had when he was young taught him to spell the word "arithmetic" by using the following mnemonic device: *A R*at *I*n *T*om's *H*ouse *M*ight *E*at *T*om's *I*ce *C*ream. He said this was drummed into his head, and he never forgot it. He had been trying to devise other mnemonics for words he felt he should know.

I told him that this would work well, especially for him since he "listened" so well internally. I also said that he could eventually learn to spell quite adequately in this way. This, however, was only provided that he was willing to spend all of his time doing nothing but this for approximately the next five hundred years. Mnemonic devices can be entertaining as well as helpful when used in a limited way. But they are extremely cumbersome and slow. I insisted that it was totally an illusion that the only way he could spell the word "arithmetic" was by using that device.

I proceeded to tell him what we had told Steve about photographic memory. I then said that all he really had to do was learn to visualize something on which he had seen the word "arithmetic" written. He replied that the last time he could think of must have been the last time he had an arithmetic book, which would have been about sixth grade. He was sure he couldn't possibly remember back that far. I told him he was wrong, and that all he had to do was look up and to his right (left and right were reversed for him) and tell me what color the book was. He said it was red. I then asked him if he could *see* what color the letters were. He said, "Yeah, sort of silver or gray." I said that, if he could see them, he could certainly read them to me from the book cover. He said, "A-R-I-T-H-M-E-T-I-C." Then he looked a little bewildered for a few moments and said, "S---, I got it right? I really *do* have photographic memory! Boy I can't wait to get home and flip out my wife with THIS one!" At that point it was simply a matter of future pacing and practice. Russ felt really good.

Experiment #7: Stretch . . .

Think of a teaching method you know of (or use one that is moderately effective but slow, cumbersome, or difficult). After reading this far, you may be able to think about this method in a new way. Break it down into some logical, component parts. Then, examine these and find out what the problem areas are. Make up replacement parts for these problem areas and reassemble this formerly cumbersome teaching method into a streamlined version.

As an alternative, imagine some totally new and different approach to teaching this subject matter. Use your creativity. Anything that works at least as well or better will provide a viable alternative for teaching. Get in the habit of having as many viable alternatives as possible.

Notes

Chapter 3

1. In NLP, this is called analog marking.
2. In his famous studies of the effects of electrical stimulation of the surface of the brain, Penfield showed that a small amount of electricity applied to the cortex, on conscious patients, caused some of them to recall experiences they thought they had forgotten. And they often remembered them in vivid detail. This does not prove the point I am making here. It simply points to an interesting possibility. For more information see: Penfield, Wilder and T. Rasmussen, *The Cerebral Cortex Of Man: A Clinical Study Of Localization Of Function* (New York: Macmillan Publishing, 1957).

CHAPTER 4

CONNECTIONS

It was a simpler time back in the days when I had a continual flow of children to experiment with. It is easy to use a private practice to practice privately, but you can't do it on as large a scale as in a crowded social services agency. I used to have the most fascinating children and parents come to see me. I used to invent and explore galore. And, using sheer simplicity, I used to get immense pleasure out of stopping bureaucratic bucks. Most of what seems really complicated and depressing is usually really simple and can be made pleasurable. (That sounds a lot like the last fortune cookie I read.)

I'll never forget a phone call I had from a scared and confused mother. Her little girl Sally had really been through the mill. She was in third grade in the regular class, but her mother told me that that wasn't the right class. Sally's mother was warned about the emotional problems Sally was going to develop any day now because she was supposed to be in the special class and she needed a social worker. That's what the tests said. Sally was flunking everything, and mother was very angry because the tests were so expensive and the psychologist's recommendations were impossible to follow, but they were supposed to be the best ones available.

(If those two sentences got you as short of breath and confused as they did me, you'll have an accurate idea of what that conversation was like.)

I asked Sally's mother to bring Sally in to see me, and we'd see what I could do to help. She said she couldn't do that. She'd have to see me herself, first.

When Sally's mother came in to see me she was rather upset. First, I tried to make her comfortable enough to explain to me, clearly, just what was going on. She wanted me to read the lengthy and very prestigious psychological report that she had brought with her. I refused on the grounds that I could probably write one just like it after spending five minutes with Sally—if I were so inclined. The tests, I told her, may be fairly accurate, but they wouldn't be of much use to me. She would just have to tell me what *she* thought was important. I told her, also, that I might be able to do a lot more than provide emotional support for her "misplaced" child.

She then started at the beginning. Sally had had problems in school from the start. After a while, her teachers discovered that she had real, physical, eye and ear problems. Over a series of months, she had several operations to correct these difficulties. As a result, she could now see and hear normally. But, she was still doing lousy in school. Sally's mother was not satisfied with the handling of the evaluation procedures by the school board. (There was generally a four to five month wait for testing and evaluation, plus a couple of months before the results could come back.) She decided to have the testing and evaluation done privately. It was quite thorough but also quite expensive. The major recommendation was a special education class of no more than eight children. The feeling was that little Sally was emotionally immature and, thus, needed more individual attention than other children. They said she was learning disabled, so there were lots of other complicated recommendations as well. *But,* due to the timing of the evaluation and to the limited choices available in the public schools, Sally was assigned to a *regular* class of twenty-five children. One ill-equipped to provide the unusual services recommended in the evaluation. So Sally's mother was told to *expect* failure, to expect emotional problems for little Sally due to frustrations and so forth. With this glum prognosis, the school suggested that she seek the help of a social worker to provide emotional support and to ease the inevitable pain ... In other words, she should surrender.

I asked Sally's mother how well Sally *liked* her current class. She said that Sally really enjoyed it. She liked the other kids and her teacher even though she was having a lot of trouble doing the work. At that point, I told her that I had heard all I needed to help Sally. I also said that I thought that as long as Sally liked her class, she should stay there. I would help her catch up. Mother thought I was kidding or nuts. I assured her that I was serious and that I could teach Sally to learn quickly and painlessly. (I was really cocky at that point.) I would also give her some exercises and experiments to do with Sally that would help even more. We made another appointment.

I thought that this work would probably be pretty easy and allow me the freedom to experiment a great deal. I figured that Sally had not had much chance to develop many workable strategies for relating visual, auditory, and kinesthetic kinds of information to each other. I also figured that part of the reason she was enjoying school, even though she had not improved academically, was that she could now at least see and hear decently. (*I* would sure have felt better if I were her.) Third, her "immaturity" was probably just an outgrowth, or artifact, from not having had the opportunity to develop understanding strategies.

I also became whimsically philosophical. One of my hobbies is studying epistemology (essentially the study of the origins and nature of knowledge itself—I have strange hobbies). I remembered the ideas of John Locke and others who believed that a human being begins life as a *tabula rasa,* or "a blank slate." Real humanness, according to this belief, comes only through experience. To take this a step further, human potential really is limited by how much can be packed onto that slate through learning. The better organized, the more he, she, or it will hold. My forte (and my goal with Sally) is to teach the organization: the how, not the how much, of learning. I remembered the old Zen saying that if you give a man a fish, you feed him for a day. But if you teach him to fish, you feed him for a lifetime.

The only surprise I had when Sally came in was her appearance. Her mother was an extremely attractive and outgoing woman. Little Sally was a pudgy little cherub with glasses and a nasal voice. She was clever and funny though. After spending a couple of minutes getting to know her, and vice versa, I asked her a few questions, such as what gave her the most trouble in school. She and her mother both agreed it was spelling. Sally had a spelling test every Friday. She had been getting four or five right each week, which was good solid failure.

Since it was so incredibly easy to teach spelling, I decided to start there and expand to other areas. I explained to Sally and her mother about visualization and how it was necessary in spelling. I also said that I bet the psychological reports said that Sally had "a deficit or inability to 'pair' auditory and visual information." Sally's mother said that was true. The psychologists had told her that was one of the main sources of Sally's problems. I told her that I knew what the report said because every psychological report I had ever read on every child with any learning problem said the same things. And, that was the main reason I didn't bother to read the damn things. I also said the usual recommendation for this "problem" was a whole bunch of games, exercises, and strange devices that were to be administered by teachers and other professionals for a couple of years, in the hope of some improvement or compensation. Mother told me this all sounded sickeningly familiar. She also mentioned something about several hundred dollars, a few all-day trips across town, considerable anguish (and a lot of other stuff that even I consider unprintable) just to find out what I had just told her (for free) in about the five minutes I had mentioned earlier.

While we were talking I was formulating an experiment. I remembered a research study on eidetic imagery (photographic memory) that I had heard about years earlier. I remembered my introductory psychology professor telling us about it, so it must have been about ten years earlier. I often find tidbits from diverse sources incredibly useful. Not because they tell me what to do, but rather, because they lead me to new possibilities.

This particular study made several interesting points. First, many children before the age of five or six have fantastically complete visual memories. Most of them "lose" it after that age.[1] Second, the study revealed something really interesting regarding visual foreground and background (gestalt, for those who are curious). The children were shown a picture on a plain white screen for a few seconds. Then the picture was turned off and they were asked to "hold it" on the screen in their minds's eyes. As long as they looked at the screen, many of them had remarkably complete memory for the picture. They were able to describe very minute details about even very complex pictures. Some of them were questioned for up to twenty minutes on details of pictures they had seen for only a few seconds. They did as well as if the picture itself were still there in front of them, not just their memory of it. But, if they "moved" the picture off the screen, they seemed to lose it. In fact, if they moved the picture toward the edge of the screen, it seemed to fall off the edge. If they moved the picture halfway off the screen, they would lose that half only. That which had remained on the screen would continue to remain.

In Sally's case, I was thinking about this in relation to the eye movement patterns. I knew that most people, when remembering a visual image, move their eyes up and left. I added to this the thought that it is easier to visualize something against a plain white background, as in the study. I also knew that, for most people, when they remember something they have heard, they move their eyes down and left. It helps internal listening. A fourth piece of information I gained from that study was that as long as the picture was held on the white background it would stay. I didn't, and still don't, believe the part about losing the *ability* after six years of age. I believe, rather, that we are taught not to use this wonderful natural ability in favor of much less effective methods of information (mis)processing (I know my cynicism is showing).

Another piece of information is important here. When someone's eyes are aimed up and to their left, though it is easy to visualize, it *can* be very difficult or even impossible to remember (or "access") *sounds.* By the same token, when looking down and left, though it is easy to internally access memories of sounds, it can be difficult or impossible for some people to visualize.

During my NLP training, we experimented with these ideas. I remember particularly some people's difficulty when looking down and to the right (which gets most people in touch with their feelings), remembering simple visual information. One man could not tell me the color of his mother's eyes, or the color of his car, while he was looking down at all. He had to move his eyes up to be able to give me information even this basic. And this has absolutely nothing to do with intelligence or capability as a person.

What does this have to do with little Sally? Everything. On a spelling test a word is spoken by the teacher. The child's job at that point is to *hear* the word, attach a visual image (internal) to the sound—visual/auditory pairing—and write the word.[2] Remember, writing is just a visual representation (a picture) of speech. It just takes a bit of physical motion to perform the transformation from sound to picture, provided there is no problem in the translation on the *inside.* If someone fails, it is usually because he or she did not attach the right picture to the right sound. Of course, if words were spelled the way they sound, they could be "sounded out." This isn't the case in the English language. So the memory of a particular picture (the correct spelling of the word) *must be* attached (anchored) to the sound of that particular word.[3]

Again, this was the knowledge I had to work with, in the context of the difficulties presented to me by Sally and her mother. Next, I asked Sally to spell a few easy words. Each time she looked lost or puzzled. She would move her eyes in several directions as if searching[4] for the answer. She would either guess, usually wrong, or forget what the word was altogether. She just didn't know how to "think" about what she was doing. This was exactly what I expected. Fortunately, she did not become terribly flustered during the process, and she still wanted to know how to do it.

I asked her a few questions to determine exactly what kind of eye movements were normal for her. (Remember, not everyone is the same.) I asked her what color her house was. Then her car, bedroom walls, and so forth. Each time, she looked up and to her left just before answering. Then I asked her about some of her favorite songs and how they sounded to her. Her eyes would go down and to the left each time, just prior to her answer. When I asked her what certain things felt like, she would access that information while looking down and to her right. These questions are pretty standard fare for a novice NLP therapist, which is what I was at the time. But I needed to make sure that I knew her naturally occurring eye movements before I could proceed.

Actually, I knew several ways (ranging from simple, obvious and direct to complex, covert, and vastly indirect) to teach Sally to connect the sounds of words to their visual image (spelling). I wanted one that was fun and simple. Also, I wanted something fast and simple to give to teachers. Third, I wanted to get Sally's mother into the process of helping her, since she was feeling so abused about the entire thing so far. I wanted to simultaneously help them both. I explained to them what Sally needed to be able to do. I explained about the eye movements and what they meant. I offered them a new experimental technique for teaching the proper sequence for spelling. (I told them the reason it was new and experimental was that I had just made it up in my head.)

I took a note pad with a plain white sheet of paper on it. I told Sally we were going to practice using the paper as a movie screen and try to "see" things on it. I also told her that she really did know how to spell, but that she didn't know she knew because nobody had taught her where to look. I said she would be able to see what she needed to on the blank page easiest if her eyes were pointed up and to her left. I had her face directly ahead and move her eyes in that direction. I held the note pad about eighteen inches from her eyes, directly in the line of her gaze. Then I asked her to see letters as I called them out on the page. Then words as I spelled them to her. Within a few minutes, she was comfortable making her own images on the page.

I asked her again to spell a couple of words for me. She began to have trouble: She could generally get the first couple of letters but didn't have the rest of the image of the word. When I asked her to tell me the word, she couldn't: she forgot it. Remember that she didn't have the whole picture of the word, and her eyes were aimed up and left. To hear the word internally, she had to look down and left. So I added another step.

As she looked at those first few letters, I told her to keep the picture on the page. I knew, provided the information in the study was correct, that she should be able to do this fairly easily. I then slowly moved the note pad—her movie screen—downward. Her eyes followed. When the pad was in the proper position for internal hearing (down and to her left) I asked her if she had held the picture. She said, "Yes." I asked her to hear the word inside her head. She was able to say the word with her eyes pointed in this direction. I had her repeat the word. Then I slowly moved the pad back to its original position: up and left. She would generally get more of the picture at this step. I repeated this process several times for each word. I simply started with the note pad at the position she normally visualized in. Then I told her the word and found out how much of it she could see. I moved the pad down to the position where she could best hear inside her head. I would continually move the pad from one spot to the other, while helping her add letters if necessary. I stopped after about twenty to twenty-five minutes because I was convinced it was working and because Sally was a little tired. I had discovered earlier that this work was quite powerful and could cause fatigue quickly. But in the long run . . .

I asked Sally's mother if she would be willing to practice with Sally at home for a couple of weeks. She said of course, but wasn't real sure what she was to do. I told her to take

Sally's spelling list for the week to start with. Sally and her mother would do the following exercise: Sally was to look at the first word carefully. Sally's mother was to hold up a plain white note card or piece of paper, up and to Sally's left, as I had done, then say the word as Sally "held" the picture on the card, and move the card from up and left to down and left. She was then to make sure Sally could hear the word inside her head as well as seeing it spelled correctly on the card. I also told her to experiment with the process.

I explained that this was how most classroom information was stored in memory. So, they were to feel free to play with the procedure as they wished. Sally could hold the card herself when she felt comfortable, while her mother called out the words. The goal of these exercises was for Sally not to need the viewing screen at all. I told them that, if they practiced a half hour each day, they could probably reach that goal in a couple of weeks or less. And that process would spread to other classroom activities as well.

I saw them again about three weeks later. On the first spelling test Sally had after that initial session, she got fourteen of sixteen correct. On the next she got all sixteen correct. I kept track for the next few weeks. She got all of her words right from then on.

As for memorization, Sally did fine from then on. In fact most of her abilities improved along with her spelling. I did no more work with her on anything except one small problem. Several weeks after I had helped her with spelling, her mother brought her in and said, "She's stuck again." I asked what the problem was. Mother said she was stuck in math and couldn't learn anything. I told her that was a bigger statement than I was willing to accept and that she would have to break it down a bit. After some discussion, it turned out that Sally was stuck on long division. Everything else was OK, but the class was spending some time on division. Since Sally wasn't getting it, it looked like she was a lot worse off than she really was.

I gave Sally a couple of problems to do. She couldn't even begin without trouble: she would put the numbers or the lines in the wrong places, making different mistakes each time. This really upset her mother, which really upset Sally. I stopped for a few minutes to calm them both down.

Then I asked Sally if she knew what division was for. She didn't. I asked a few more basic questions to determine if she had any concept about what division was or its relationship to addition, subtraction, and multiplication. She had no idea what I was talking about. As I watched her, I realized that she was again searching around in her head and coming up blank. I decided to draw her a picture.

I thought about pictures of pies with slices taken out, á la Montessori (and Sara Lee—I used to get hungry in math class as a kid). As I thought about it, I decided this wasn't quite to the point. Sally was comfortable with addition, subtraction, and multiplication. Indeed, she was comfortable with numbers as long as her mother didn't get angry or upset.

I also knew that mathematics is really an artificial system, devised by man. But it's a pretty useful one. Once you can understand how different processes within it make up the whole form, it gets easy. This is holistic (from whole) thinking. It is what Sally didn't have for division. She knew what steps to take, that is, the sequence of events. But without the whole picture, the sequence was meaningless to her. Besides, her nervousness kept her from getting the picture.

So I decided to forgo pies and stick with numbers. I wanted to keep her as relaxed as possible the whole time she was learning. I sent mother out of the room. Next I wrote the number 111. I asked Sally if she knew how many ones were in 111. She didn't really understand, which was sort of what I expected. So I drew the following diagram:

$$100$$
$$10$$
$$1$$

I pointed to the one and asked how many ones were there. She said one. Then I pointed to the ten and asked how many ones were there. She looked puzzled for a second then said ten. I repeated with the 100. Then I went on to explain that if you added:

$$
\begin{array}{r}
100 \\
+\ 10 \\
+\ \ 1 \\
\hline
=111.
\end{array}
$$

you got

I then explained to her that I had just shown her a kind of division. We had just divided 111 into hundreds, tens, and ones to see how many ones would fit into it. I saw a glimmer of understanding. I then spent about ten minutes showing her how to add up the ones, tens, and hundreds, how to multiply the ones by tens, tens by tens, and so forth, and what would happen if we subtracted some from the total. I showed her addition, subtraction, and multiplication, based on the number 111. Then I showed her how to divide with other numbers, using some of the same examples. Within a half an hour of work she understood what she was doing. She was able to divide.

Then I spent some time showing her mother what we had done. I asked her if anyone had ever done that for her when she was Sally's age. She said no but she wished they had. I said she could help make up for it by helping Sally with this kind of explanation whenever she needed it. It was at that point that she really understood that Sally was all right. Sally never had suffered from a learning disability.

Notes

Chapter 4

1. Some people associate this loss with the completion of myelinization that occurs in a child's brain at about the same age. "Myelinization" describes a process in which fatty sheaths grow around the cells in the cortex, turning them into white matter instead of gray matter. This speeds up the electrical activity along each cell.

    These theorists do not make the more obvious correlation: the loss of this ability occurs at the same time that formal education, with its prescribed processes of learning, begins.
2. Writing itself is a complex task, but those complexities are not germane here.
3. We usually distinguish similar sounding words from each other by the context in which they appear. On a spelling test this is taken care of ahead of time.
4. This process is called transderivational search.

CHAPTER 5

LATER ON

There are several ways to help or teach someone. You can treat people as if they are on an assembly line in which the same thing is done to everyone in the same way. Results are measured and counted at the end of the line. All that matters are the percentages. If they look good, the process rolls along. If they don't look so good, you change up, retool, and start again. You just keep counting and measuring.

A much better way is to think in individual terms. Then you do what people need, rather than what *you* always do. If each person you meet presents you with a challenge, or a series of challenges, you get to be creative. For each challenge you can set up a new experiment and see what happens.

The nice thing about an experiment is that there are no bad results. Just learning. For each of the people I work with, I set up experiments to see what will happen right in front of me. If the person I am trying to help gets something worthwhile out of the experiment, fine. If not, we set up another experiment. Knowing what won't work is often at least as valuable as knowing what will.

Aside from immediate results in the office, new patterns often stick in the person's behavior. When I was working with the people described in this book, I would do three to six month follow-up calls to make sure the changes lasted for at least that long. Generally, if new behavior lasts past three months, that's good enough. It is seldom that people will slip back into the old patterns unless some major trauma occurs. For Russ, Pen, and Sally, I waited until I had written to this point, to call them for a second followup. I knew that they had done fine for months after I saw them. But now it was several years later. I had no doubt that they would remember me. Also, I was sure they would remember what I had taught them. I was curious, though, to see if what I had taught them had become a normal part of their ongoing behavior. I also wondered what *other* changes were generated by the work we did.

Before we go back to discussing Russ, Pen, and Sally, there is one other person we need to remember: Josh. True, he had stopped running away altogether, but I had many uneasy feelings about the whole affair. I was essentially waiting for what we had done to either backfire completely or not to last. As is often the case, I got sort of a combination.

I wrote Josh's mother a letter, asking her to call me. When she did, she told me he had run away again. I asked her to be more specific, and we had the following conversation:

Her: We went over to the laundromat, and I told him to sit in that chair and be quiet. Then he ran out the door.

Me: Wait a minute. How long did he sit in the chair?

Her: About 20 minutes.

Me: How long did you expect him to?

Her: Well, the laundry takes 2–3 hours.

Me: What did you have for him to do? Did you bring some books, or toys, or something for him?

Her: Nope.

Me: (with probably too irate a tone in my voice) Did you just expect him to sit quietly in a chair for 2–3 hours without anything to keep him occupied?

Her: He's supposed to do what I say.

Me: He lasted longer in that chair than I would have! Twenty minutes is great with a setup like that.

We then had a short, somewhat circular discussion about expectations: reasonable versus ridiculous. I then asked about his behavior in school. Her answer was something like the following:

Her: I don't send him to school now.
Me: Why not?
Her: He'll just run away.
Me: But he hasn't run away from school since I saw him!
Her: It doesn't matter, he will.
Me: But, but . . . .

We continued in another short loop until I finally insisted that she send him to school. I told her that she would just have to, that it was the law, and so forth. She agreed that she would. She also agreed that she would arrange things for him to do when she took him places, to see if it helped him stay put.

She called me again a couple of weeks later as we had prearranged. I asked if she had sent Josh to school. She said she was going to take him to school one day but it rained, and she hadn't gotten around to it yet, and the holidays were coming, and . . . We made an appointment for after the holidays. I intended to ask her some pretty direct questions when I saw her in person.

Not only did she fail to show up for her appointment, but she started avoiding me. She answered neither the letters I sent her nor the messages sent through the outreach worker at the project. After several weeks of this, I called the school social worker and the outreach worker. I told them to go over to the place Josh and his mother were living, and *bring* him to school themselves, or whatever they thought was appropriate once they got there.

Two days later, the school social worker called me back with the following report:

Sid, we went out there, but it was real strange. We *knew* she was home with Josh and her baby. But she wouldn't answer the door. We even saw her peeking through the window, so she knew who we were. It was spooky, so we left. What do you think we ought to do?

"Call child protection," was my reply. We had a short discussion and agreed that we had seen enough of the subtle signs of child abuse to call in the authorities. There was nothing else we could do at that point. Josh's mother's refusal to send him to school was grounds enough to do *something,* anyway.

The outreach worker had told me earlier that Josh's mother had complained to her about Josh's behavior at home, particularly with the man she was living with. When I asked her about the conversations they had had, she said that Josh's mother had been letting her know that it was coming down to a choice between the man and Josh. She also made it clear that Josh would lose that battle. We filled in the other pieces of the puzzle in our heads, but they aren't relevant here. The child protection agency handled it from there.

In retrospect, there were several things to learn from working with Josh. My original hypothesis was that if I paced and led Josh properly, I could get him to change his behavior immediately: to stop running away. My hypothesis was correct. My second hypothesis was that there was a good reason for him to be running away and that it would become apparent if I paid attention. This one was also correct. But it took months to confirm it and handle the situation in a useful fashion. I had been advised several times to close the case, because Josh's mother was so uncooperative. But I am an ornery fellow. I felt that it was worthwhile to pursue. I still do.

I visited with Pen and his grandmother the other day. When I first met Pen he was twelve and a half. He is now about seventeen. I had high hopes that in the meantime he had made significant progress in school. I began by asking about his behavior. His grandmother told me that he had been skipping classes the past few months and she was concerned that this was an indication of behavior problems in general. I asked her about her own worries about Pen.

Grandma: And like I tell him, they got nothin' but trouble out there. Boys stealing, using dope, doing everything. He could be coming along the street and just get hurt for nothing!

Sid: Let me ask you something. Has he really gotten into any trouble so far?

Grandma: No, he never did.

Sid: Not a bit, huh?

Grandma: No, he never did.

Sid: Not a bit, huh?

Grandma: Not a bit.

In fact, as we talked further, it became apparent that Pen is unusually well behaved. He hasn't had a single fight since the day I met him. She and I discussed this, and she felt reassured that, since he had so far managed to avoid the fights, crimes, drugs, and trouble that he was surrounded by, he was probably going to continue to do so. Then I wanted to find out about academics.

Sid: (To Pen) You remember when we did all that funny stuff, right? Have you been able to read any better since then?

Pen: Not that good.

Sid: Not that good, huh. Did you do any better than you did before?

Pen: Uh, huh (nods yes).

Sid: But, you still don't read as good as you want to.

Pen: No, I wanna read good.

I then asked him to read the labels on a couple of things on their kitchen table. He couldn't. Pen, his grandma, and I then talked about his frustration in class and about getting help from teachers. He was very clear about his difficulty in reading and his teachers' unwillingness, or inability, to help him. The thought of him going into tenth grade next year without knowing how to read was mind boggling. At that point Grandma handed me some report cards and papers.

Grandma: This is some more, the reports. They're bad, very bad. I be ashamed when it comes. Very, very, very bad. (She shakes her head sadly.)

Sid: Don't be ashamed, now. It sound to me like, you know, when he asks for help, they're not going to give it to him.

Grandma: I know . . . You know, if he could spell, it seems like he could be able to read better. But, he just can't.

Sid: Yes, he can. I can teach him to spell in fifteen minutes.

Grandma: Yeah?

Sid: How long did it take me to teach him the alphabet and how to relax in school?

Grandma: *No* time!

Sid: That's right. Spelling's just as easy.

I then took Pen through the spelling strategy, exactly as it is explained in the tear-out section of this book. He was able to spell words that he hadn't seen, heard, or understood before. He spelled them backwards and forwards, in about five minutes. Then he ran to get his brother, so I could teach him too. We discussed math and the use of the same mechanisms for multiplication tables, and so on.

Grandma: This boy went to start school when he was four years old and eight months. And, I say "darn." It looks like all your life is going to school, and ain't nothing coming out!

Sid: They just don't know how to do it. You know every time I sat down with him and taught him something, he learned it like that!

Grandma: Like that (snaps fingers).

Sid: Do you think he's slow?

Grandma: No.

Sid: He's not slow.

Grandma: I know.

Sid: He's not.

Grandma: They don't want to have the patience, neither.

They just mark him right down "bad." No attention or nothing like that. They don't help the kids.

We then talked about what to do. I told her that the teachers had obviously given up on Pen a long time ago and that none of them had any intentions of sitting down with him and teaching him. We all agreed that it was up to them to make sure Pen learned what he needed. My original sadness and disgust was renewed. It was very painful to tell a sixty-eight-year-old woman that teaching her grandson to read would be *her* responsibility. I told her I would help when I could. (What a shame.)

I went straight from Pen's home over to see Russ and his wife. We talked about old stories and how life was going for them, for a while. Then I told him about this book and what I was doing.

Sid: What I'm interested in is how you're doing with your
    reading.
Russ: Uh.
Sid: Do you work on it?
Russ: To be honest with you, I haven't had the time to really
    get into it . . . I can understand some things—like, my
    brother, he had sent over these, uh (hands me a volume
    that is a yearbook from a very difficult encyclopedia).
Sid: Can you read this (not believing)?
Russ: No. Some things I can, like, this issue here: Elvis
    Presley's death is in here, like an obituary . . .

At this point he turned to that section of the volume and began reading to me. He read flawlessly, only faltering over three or four of the longest words. I helped him with those, but it was immediately clear to me that his reading was much better than it had been. He told me that he was able to read the newspaper as well as he wants. He couldn't when I had last seen him. I remarked on his improvement and his wife agreed. He read at a comfortable pace, without tension, breathing normally.

Sid: Sounds pretty good to me.

Russ: Still a little rusty around the edges (wife laughs).

Sid: How much better is that than the way he read 3 years ago?

Wife: You know I've had a seventh grade education, and there's words that I stumble over myself. So everybody's not perfect. You could have a high-school education and you'd still stumble over words.

Russ: I know a word when I *hear* it. She'll say a word, and she won't pronounce it right, and I'll tell her how to pronounce it right, because I've *heard* that word before. Big words.

We spent some time practicing spelling and showing Russ's daughter how to visualize properly. We talked some more about Russ's remarkable auditory memory, and how much fun he has with it.

Russ: . . . I'm doing better, not great, but . . .

Sid: You're pretty hard on yourself, because you're really doing all right.

Russ: Well, I figure if I be hard on myself, I'll do better. The harder I am, the better I'll get.

Sid: All right, I'll go along with that. You might be right.

Russ: If I say to myself, "Now you're doing great," then you tend to relax—a little *too* much. Then you end up right back where you was, and it takes you that much longer to get started again. So this way, you know, I keep it up there, try harder.

Sid: Well, if it makes you try harder, keep it up.

Wife: After he used to come home from seeing you, he'd talk about what you had showed him. It was really remarkable that he could just make a picture in his head and spell. He picked it up like that, right off the bat.

I was thoroughly pleased at this point with the progress Russ had made. His motivation strategy was to be negative and hard on himself. But as long as it worked this well, I left it alone. Russ's parting comments were something about getting drunk together the next time we . . .

I called Sally's mother a couple of weeks ago. It had been nearly three years since I had spoken with her. We talked for a short while and got caught up. The family had had a series of tragedies and a string of deaths, so times have been hard for them. I told her what I was doing and why I had called.

> Sid: How is Sally doing in school now? I know things have been tough but I'm wondering if she has been improving.
>
> Mother: Sid, you would be so proud of her, she's really doing well. She's had some problems, of course, but so would you if you couldn't hear or see straight for nine years. (laughs).
>
> Sid: Objectively, how much of a help was I back then?
>
> Mother: Oh, she couldn't have done it without you. I mean, you set her right on the right track. You were exactly what she needed.

She went on to praise the school Sally is in. It really is a model public school. The staff, some of whom I know, are really dedicated. They believe in developing the whole child rather than just pumping children with information.

When I went to visit them, Sally's mother pulled out her files. She had literally journals full of information on everything from her feelings and thoughts, to Sally's school records, test papers, and on and on. She remarked about her own compulsiveness and attention to detail. I praised her for her energy and commented on the amount of stress she could handle. I also suggested she ease up on herself. She told me that she had finally gotten her own high-school diploma in the three years we hadn't seen each other.

I asked her about comments from Sally's teachers. She said that her present teacher is amazed at how well Sally does, considering her history. He said she progresses rapidly and works hard to improve. She reads fluently though she has

CHAPTER 6
TEACHING TEACHING

Recent years have seen some strange priority shifts in the field of education, with some resulting backlash. The Sixties and most of the Seventies were full of early screening programs galore. Immense amounts of money and time were spent trying to find as many medical, psychological, and social problems as anyone could dream up. Grant money went in the direction of diagnostic aids of all types. Teachers and kids shuffled in and out of doctors' and therapists' offices looking for all kinds of deficiencies. After ten or fifteen years of all this progress, things were at least as bad, if not far worse than ever before. So the reactions had to happen. *Back to basics.* In other words, let's do what we did before. But, wait a minute. We stopped doing what we did before because it wasn't real terrific. This is progress?

The victims are as much the teachers as the students. Teacher education is extremely vast, but not that usable: tons of theory, little practicality. And nobody can make up their mind about what is best for kids.

That is why teachers have so much continuing education. About every teacher I have ever met is still in school and attending countless workshops and seminars. As far as I can tell, and I've done an awful lot of asking, they learn the same stuff over and over again! Teachers are supposed to be flexible. They are supposed to make good contact with children and speak the same language as the kids. They are supposed to shape the children's behavior, but only within the limits of whatever developmental model is in vogue. In addition, special education teachers are supposed to keep up with the latest advances, newest screening instruments, teaching aids, games, devices, and so forth. I've asked a bunch of them if they use those thousands of games and things. The last one told me, "No, and the closet is so full of the damn things there is no room for any coats!"

Under this barrage of obvious or useless information and junk, there are countless teachers burning out at an early age. They know their education is inadequate. They know the theories are impractical. They know that 40% of the children aren't brain damaged. They want help.

It seems to me that one of the areas of really weak teacher education is in useful communication skills. I know teachers go to lots of seminars on communication, but that isn't what I'm talking about. Are teachers taught "platform skills" or "stage presence?" Are they taught to organize information in a way that fits in with the sensory/neurological organization of the children? Are they taught foolproof ways of establishing rapport with a child or group? Are they taught group dynamics in a way that will help them get kids to cooperate and help one another? Are they taught ways of heightening their own sensory acuity so that they really perceive what is happening in front of them? Are they taught models of organizing their behavior that will literally teach them how to be flexible? I don't think teachers are taught any of those things. But these are central to teaching effectively.

This chapter is about how to learn those things. This book will not teach you. It will structure your thinking, so that you can learn, however, and you'll learn by doing. You can read this chapter in minutes; *doing* this chapter will take longer. Doing these experiments will make you a better teacher. Much better than the reading of them. This chapter is divided into sections: each is designed to help you learn progressively more useful skills. Each section includes a good deal of explanation and three experiments: the first is quite easy. The second is less easy, the third is the most advanced. None of them is hard. Some take more time than others. Different people will find different things in each. Sounds like life, doesn't it? Happy exploring!

Platform Skills

We have all watched a wide variety of performers in action. We go to concerts, movies, and plays. We watch TV, listen to records, tapes, and the radio, and we know what is entertaining to us personally. Usually, if we watch/listen to a particular performance we have a sense of whether or not we like it, within the first few minutes. I wonder if many of us have ever taken the time to figure out how we make up our minds.

It is interesting to me that there are so many different things certain types of performers have to do. Comedians George Carlin, Rodney Dangerfield, and Joan Rivers have to make people laugh.

Johnny Carson has to do that and much more. He has to be able to interview a variety of people. If he is talking with Rodney Dangerfield, he has to be a straight man. If he is talking with someone who isn't used to being on TV, he has to make them feel comfortable, get them to talk about themselves, and create an attitude in the audience—perhaps curiosity or warmth. If he is interviewing the author of a book (generally in the last few minutes of the show) he may have to first change the pace of the show, then create an attitude of interest and respect for the guest, gather general information about his or her work, and make some pertinent point about the subject. At the same time, he has to sell the book! No matter what's going on, Johnny is still expected to be clever, smooth, and funny. The audience doesn't much care how he's feeling that particular day. They'll expect his best.

The same goes for news people, politicians, actors, and others who communicate directly to an audience. However, there is a whole class of communicators who don't even get the opportunity to confront their audience: a conductor faces his orchestra, but holds his *back* to his audience. He has to trust that his skill at getting a large number of musicians to watch him, listen to themselves, read the music, cooperate with one another, and act as a single entity will convey a message to the audience. The amazing thing is that it's almost always someone else's message! No conductor will ever have the opportunity to check with Beethoven or Mozart to make sure he got it straight.

At least the conductor gets to turn around right after he's finished and find out how he did. Just think of the job of a film director: when he's done shooting, he still has to wait months, or even years, before anyone sees what he's accomplished.

If you are saying to yourself, "I'm beginning to understand some parallels between teaching and performing," congratulations! If not, you're still in luck. You have an opportunity to look at your profession in a fun, new way.

We can start by setting up a framework for comparison. We then pick a type of performer, the stand-up comic, for instance, as a model. To some teachers, the analogy is closer than to others, but we'll just let that stand. Then we can look more closely at the steps each one goes through while performing. To narrow ourselves down, we can compare the delivery of a monologue to the delivery of a lesson, step by step.

The first thing to be aware of is that, even before the comic or teacher starts, many important things have already happened. For the comic, the stage has already been set, literally. The audience comes with a set of expectations. The comic already has his assignment: make people laugh. The same is true for the teacher: the classroom already exists. The children come with a set of expectations also. So the teacher has an assignment as well: help children learn. The extent to which each has the preexisting ability to perform flexibly and effectively and to meet the audience's expectations will determine the extent to which he or she can fulfill the respective assignments.

Once on stage, or in class, the actual task begins. We can break this down into four steps. The first step for each is *building rapport.* This is pacing, as I have described throughout this book. For the comic telling a joke, it is the "setup." He or she begins to tell a story that people in the audience can relate to. As he or she tells this, he or she hopes that expectation, curiosity, and understanding will build in the audience. For the teacher, the task is quite similar. He or she will begin to tell some story or explain some process. The steps in a math problem are a good example of this. Again, there should be a building of expectation, curiosity, and understanding. These feelings for both the comic and the teacher bring the watchers, listeners, or both closer, not only to him or her but also to each other. It's that group feeling that is so important.

The second step is *leading*. For the comic, this is the punch line: usually, some twisted conclusion to his story. His purpose is to be funny enough to get people to laugh. For the teacher, this is some sort of conclusion drawn from the information he or she has presented: this can be the point to the story or the answer to a math problem. The purpose is to be clear enough so that children understand, know, or can do something new.

The third step is *attending*. At this point, both the comic and teacher have to pause a moment for their audiences to respond. The comic listens for laughter. He also watches for facial expression and other cues from the audience. If people are smiling and appear to be enjoying themselves—big fun; if they are yawning and looking at their watches—big trouble. The teacher listens for comments or questions regarding what he or she has just presented. He or she also watches facial expressions and other subtle hints from the children. If the children seem contented, interested, and alert—good job; if they look confused, worried, and lost—good luck.

The fourth step is further *building*. Here, the comic or teacher uses the responses, the feedback, to build on what has been done. For the comic who has gotten a big laugh, he or she keeps rolling in the same direction. Perhaps more jokes in the same vein. They will bring the audience even closer and create more fun. If however, the joke didn't go over, he or she might slyly comment on the failure in a way that might get a laugh. Then the experienced comic will try something in a different vein: go back to step one. The teacher who got his or her message across can expand on the idea or give further examples or assignments. He or she can answer questions and comments and dialogue in a useful way with students. If, however, the teacher perceives a major lack of understanding or a large amount of head scratching—back to step one. The experienced teacher will explain the problem, or story, in a different way.

We have established, then, a convenient four-step model for both stand-up comedy and teaching (easy, huh?): (1) building rapport, (2) leading, (3) attending, (4) building. We can call this the "BLAB model." The nice thing about models is that you can call them whatever you want when you make them up. BLAB is, after all, what comics and teachers actually do. Some just do it better than others.

You may be saying at this point, "OK, Sid, jokes aside, this four-step pattern seems too simple." Of course it is! All models and analogies are simplifications. That is why we use them. None of them is perfectly accurate, either. In NLP, we constantly remind ourselves that the map is not the territory.

With this limitation in mind, I'll get back up on my high horse for a moment and slyly divulge a major difference between comics and teachers. Any experienced comic who gets no response, even to his best stuff, will take responsibility for it. I've never heard George Carlin accuse anybody in an audience of having "dyshumoria, the dreaded laughter disability." I don't expect to, either. He is much too creative for that!

As I get down off my horse, I am aware that there are lots of other comparisons between teachers and performers. Some are obvious; others are quite subtle. It is always that way when we talk about communication: there are so many ways to explore, understand, and talk about it. As you bear that in mind, the following exercise will give you a chance to try your hand at modeling.

Modeling Experiment #1

Step 1

Pick an entertainer of whom you are particularly fond of. To make it easy on yourself, you might choose someone who is on TV regularly. There are many talk shows that give you the opportunity to watch and listen to the same person at least several times each week. The same is true for newscasters and, to a lesser extent, actors in weekly series. There are also the Sunday morning TV clergymen, some of whom are very interesting, from a purely communication standpoint.

Step 2

As you watch this person, notice unique features in his or her physical behavior. These are the ones, we generally say, that make that person who he or she is. Watch for specific physical movements. For example:

1. unusual postures
2. specific hand movements
3. head turns
4. leaning to one side
5. rocking back and forth or side to side
6. facial expression (mouth and especially eyebrows)
7. movement

(It may help to turn off the sound for a few minutes and just watch.) You will find these to be very obvious most of the time. Remember the way Jack Benny held his arms? Or the way he walked? These were his trademarks. They make up much of our memory of him.

Step 3

Now listen for particularly unique features in the person's voice. Things to listen for include:

1. particular words or phrases
2. unusual sentence structure
3. voice quality and pitch
4. tone
5. volume, inflection
6. resonance (nasal, breathy)
7. speed, tempo (rhythmic, choppy)

Again, it may help to only listen. You can turn away from the set or turn down the picture for a few moments. Try also to pay less attention to what this person is talking about than normal. We're not interested so much in what he or she is saying as in how it is being said. You will undoubtedly find many obviously unique features here as well. Remember the sound of Walter Cronkite, John F. Kennedy, or Martin Luther King, Jr.? These men all had their own unique sound and were immensely powerful and influential.

Step 4

Now comes the tricky part. Here you want to find the patterns into which these sights and sounds are organized. Pick something you have seen or heard that struck you as somehow special. See if this occurs at certain times only and, perhaps, never at all. Maybe several of these features occur simultaneously. You'll know if it is repeated in the same way often, you have found a real pattern. You will know that you understand this pattern well when you can predict it moments before it happens.

This task seems obtuse for some people. An example may help. As Johnny Carson switches topics during his monologue, he generally looks over to his right, where his production staff and Ed McMahon are. He will usually turn to his left and deliver the introductory line of his next joke.

Setting up his joke, he will, almost invariably, alternate his stance: sometimes directing his lines to his right, sometimes to his left. When he gets to the punch line, however, he will often look straight ahead and deliver it directly into the camera. Changes in his hand movements, facial expressions, tone of voice, volume, and inflection all correspond to this pattern as well. When you have played with this experiment for a while, answer the following questions:

1. Was this totally mind boggling? If so, you were probably trying to relate too many things to each other at once. Go back to smaller chunks.
2. Was it easier for you to do the visual portions? Was step 3 easier? What does this tell you about your ability to

attend to one portion of your experience as opposed to another?

3. Do you have a new appreciation of what we mean when we say that someone has a particular style?

4. Do you think this might be a useful and fun experiment for other people who are professional communicators? How about for school children?

Modeling Experiment #2

When you feel you understand the patterns you have found in this powerful communicator, duplicate them. Stand in front of a full-length mirror and see if you can match that person's precise movements. Do the same with your voice by talking or reading something into a tape recorder. When you think you have it, answer the following questions:

1. Can you duplicate these motions and sounds smoothly and naturally?

2. How do you feel as you do this: awkward? surprised? confident?

3. Can you achieve a comfortable blend of that person's style and yours?

4. Does this show you areas in your own style that are rigid or limiting in some way?

Modeling Experiment #3

This is where you find out how brave and flexible you can be. Take this new style to school with you. Try it out on your classes. Be a bit subtle. If you exaggerate too much, you'll come across as a caricature of that other person. Leave that to Rich Little, he gets paid for it. Then, answer the following questions:

1. Did the children realize or figure out what you were doing?

2. Did they respond to you, or each other, differently? Did they understand better?

3. Did you notice certain parts of this new style that seemed to effect the class more than others? Did some fall flat?
4. Would you be inclined to use this style more often?
5. Would you like to try it all over again, choosing another performer? Go ahead!

This modeling process is the basis of NLP. It was developed by people who were experts in picking out the details that make up the whole of a person's communication style. They studied very powerful, effective, and influential people to duplicate their styles. They then found they could create the same effect, and of course get the same responses, as those gifted individuals. In NLP, we call this *stealing behavior*. It is not against the law: steal from the best!

Listening Skills

Besides general platform skills, there are many quite specific ways of making effective contact with people. The last exercise was designed to help you find usable patterns in the communication of people who are especially effective and swipe them. I hope you also learned something about some of the general patterns in your own communication. This will give you the opportunity to add or subtract from your own behavior as you think necessary to make yourself even more effective.

Pacing is very important for a teacher. He or she must know what to pace, or watch for, in a child's behavior in order to establish rapport with that child. This task can be almost overwhelming. This is as difficult as watching the TV actor was: there is so much going on that it becomes hard to sort out. You have to "chunk down" your thinking to a level that is both useful and manageable to be able to pace.[1]

Besides this, though, there is leading. Teachers have to do more than match and pace their students. They also can lead the kids in more useful directions. It is important that a teacher be aware of how to send a message to a child, but it is just as important to help that child be able to receive a variety of different kinds of messages.

The importance of listening effectively is almost too obvious to mention. Except that most listening programs I have been exposed to don't really train you to do anything. Typical is the task of listening to someone talk and later having to answer questions about what he or she said. As I pointed out earlier, that is the least interesting portion of communication: the content. It is important to be able to do that task effectively, but a score on a listening test is not likely to add to your skill. It is more useful to know the patterns underlying what you do or do not hear. Then you can correct deficiencies and improve your skills.

Just as important as knowing what you hear and understand (or not) is knowing the same about the kids you teach. If you know what they hear and understand, you can pace them by using that kind of information. If you know the kind of information they do not hear or understand, you can lead them into understanding it. You simply need to know how to listen.

The most useful place to start is in hearing and identifying representational systems. This informtion is contained in the predicates of people's speech. Again, this means listening to the child's words in a way that tells you which part of his sensory experience—seeing, hearing, feeling, tasting, or smelling—he is using in his speech. This will force you to pay closer attention (listening) to exactly what children tell you. In addition, you will get higher quality information. You will know more about how the child thinks if you know more about to which portion of his experience he or she pays attention. The following exercise will help you develop your skills in this area.

Listening Experiment #1

Step 1

Choose a child who is having some sort of difficulty in class and who may appear to you to have trouble understanding, communicating, or behaving in some way. For this exercise, it really doesn't matter what the trouble is. Find a relatively private place in which you can spend some time with this child —ten or fifteen minutes.

Step 2

Ask this child open-ended questions, that is, ones that require more than a nod of the head for an answer. Use predicates that are unspecific regarding sensory functioning. In other words, do not guide his or her answers into a particular representational system. If you ask a child how he or she *feels* about school, he or she will probably answer you in the same representational system, *feeling* or kinesthetic. The question, "Do you *see* some problems in class?" asks for a *seeing* answer, one that is in the visual representational system.

The following are more examples of sentences that specifically guide the child to certain representational systems for his or her answer.

1. Are you getting the *hang* of this material?
2. How do you *feel* about class?
Sentences 1 and 2 ask for a feeling response from the child.

3. Do you *see* any problems in school?
4. Do you *appear* to be progressing satisfactorily?
Sentences 3 and 4 ask for a seeing response from the child.

5. Can you *tone* down your excitement a little?
6. Is this material *clear* to you?
Sentence 5 asks for a hearing response from the child, while sentence 6 can be either visual, auditory, or, to a lesser extent, kinesthetic. People can see, hear, or feel "clearly".

An *unspecified* way of asking questions might be the following:

Are you *understanding* the material well enough?
Are you *having* any special problems or difficulties in class?
If you *wanted* to *change* anything here, what might it be?
Is there anything special you'd *like help* with?

Here are some partial lists of specified and unspecified verbs. Look them over until you understand the idea. For a longer list, see tear-out page 7.

visual	auditory	kinesthetic	unspecified
see	hear	feel	know
observe	listen	hold	believe

view	tell	touch	understand
imagine	tone	grab	remember
look	speak		have

Step 3

Get the child to talk about his or her difficulty. As you converse, listen for the predicates he or she uses. Often, when a child, or anyone, is having a problem, their speech is limited to one representational system within the context of that problem.

Step 4

As you and this child talk, switch your own predicates to his or her representational system. Continue to discuss this problem in the same representational system as this child for about five to ten minutes. When you have finished this, answer the following questions:

1. What happens when you listen for predicates? Are they easy to pick out?
2. Did you find this child to be stuck in only one representational system?
3. What happens when you switch to this representational system? Do you seem to make better contact with this child? Does the child respond to you differently?
4. Is it hard for you to switch to this representational system and maintain it?

Listening Experiment #2

Find another child who is having some sort of difficulty. Repeat the steps above which were:

(1) ask open-ended questions, using unspecified verbs,
(2) get the child to talk about his or her difficulties in class,
(3) identify the representational system the child is primarily using, and
(4) match, or pace the child.

Step 5

When you feel you have established a good rapport with this child, using the same representational system, gently switch your speech to another representational system. The following illustrates how this can be done with a child who uses visual predicates:

"OK, I really do *see* better what is happening. But I'm wondering as you *look* over the situation just how you *feel* about it?"

With a child you're using auditory predicates with, perhaps:

"I really *hear* you now, but I'm wondering if you can *imagine* any way out of this problem."

Continue the discussion for a few more minutes, maintaining the representational system you switched to. Then stop and answer the following questions:

1. Was it easy or difficult for you to switch to a new representational system once you established rapport with the child?
2. What did the child do? Did he or she get lost or confused?
3. When you switched to a new representational system, did it seem to break the contact you had established? Did the child switch with you?

Listening Exercise #3

Choose yet another child having difficulty. Go through all the steps of experiments number 1 and number 2. This time, your goal is to lead the child into a new representational system. After you switch to a new representational system, listen closely and give the child a few moments to switch also. If he or she does, fine. If not, go back and make sure that you are pacing effectively in the child's original representational system. Then gently switch again. Continue this process until the child switches with you and seems to be able to describe experiences in both the old and the new representational system. If time permits, you might try to switch again so that you and the child can communicate in the three major representational systems: visual, auditory, and kinesthetic. Then answer the following questions:

1. Was it easy for you to get the child to switch? If not, were you able to *lead* the child after a few tries?
2. When the child switched representational systems, did it improve the contact between you?
3. Did you notice other changes, either in the child or yourself, when you switched? How about changes in breathing, posture, tone of voice, rate or rhythm of speech, and so forth?
4. Do your feelings about the discussion or the child change when you do this experiment?
5. Does this seem to expand your and the child's awareness of the difficulties you discussed? Do you find that you, and/or the child are better able to handle them?

These experiments are elementary NLP devices. They will teach you to listen for a particular portion of speech. This is a very useful level to start with for one particular reason: if you found a pattern in the way the students you worked with represent experience, and whether or not they are good students there is something you need to seriously consider. Perhaps you are only effectively teaching students who use the same representational system you do. If so, you are in luck. It only takes a bit of practice to be able to systematically switch systems and add to your flexibility as a teacher.

This is still only one way of listening; there are a variety of ways to hear language, beyond the meaning of the words. Our language has many internal structures and levels. Based on a branch of linguistics known as transformational grammar, Bandler and Grinder developed a tool called the Meta-Model. It is designed to help you quickly and easily understand how a person translates internal experience into language. Once mastered, it can be used to lead people in more useful directions of thought. Though not necessary for the purposes of this book, I suggest you pick up *The Structure of Magic,* Vol. I and II for a thorough explanation of the Meta-Model. For a brief synopsis of the Meta-Model, see Appendix II. It will increase your skill as a communicator immensely.

Besides the language someone uses, there is a whole range of patterns in speech that can help you and the children you work with to communicate more effectively. For example, when someone shifts their voice tone to a higher pitch than usual, it generally indicates internal visualization. On the other hand a shift to a lower tone often means a shift to feelings. A sing-song, rhythmic voice usually indicates auditory internal accessing. Listening for shifts in pitch, tempo, timbre, volume, and so forth in the speech children use can give you similar information about them. It will also give you more levels on which to pace your students.

Watching Skills

Did you ever hear of someone offering a course to improve your watching ability? I never did. Long ago, people realized that we just don't listen very well. But most assume that we see just fine. This is especially true in our highly visually oriented society. Personally, I don't think we see all that well. If we did, someone would have discovered the eye-movement patterns I described earlier a long time ago. No one did.

The eye-movement patterns are only one part of the story of our unawareness. There are many physical movements that are highly characteristic of a person's ongoing internal experiences. That's why people talk and write books about body language. But most of the work done in that area has been done at far too gross a level of analysis. Statements such as "if someone leans back when they talk to you, they don't like you" are too general. Sometimes ridiculous. Even if something like that were true in a particular case, what do you do about it? Go home and cry, I suppose. At any rate, body language can be very important. To make it useful, we should keep our observations as specific as possible. Eye movements are a good place to start.

Watching Experiment Number 1

Step 1

Notice how kids' eyes move when they talk or listen to you (see pp. 38, 39, 40). Tear out the chart in the back (tear-out page 1) to remind you of the patterns. Asking the questions on the tear-out will help you. You can do this with one child or a group. It doesn't matter. If you find a child that doesn't seem to fit the model, which is unlikely but possible, great! You have an opportunity to use your eyes to find out how he or she is organized. Everyone has some sort of internal organization. Find it. Most importantly, *do not stare,* just watch.

Step 2

When you feel fairly confident that you can recognize accessing cues, choose a particular child you feel comfortable with. Have a conversation with this child, and make yourself aware of the pattern of his or her eye movements. For example, if the child continually looks up just prior to speaking, he or she is probably accessing an internal, visual image and then talking about it in some way. Listen to your own speech. You may find that you are using the same representational system in your speech that this child accesses in his, or her, own. If this is a child you get along well with, it is possible that you are talking directly to his or her internal pictures.

Step 3

Now pick a child you do not get along with particularly well. Do the same as above. If you find yourself talking in a different representational system than the child accesses in, switch to the one the child is using. Then answer the following questions:

1. Is it easy to watch eye movements and pick out patterns? Does it make you dizzy?

2. Do you find either of these children to be stuck in one pattern?
3. What happens when you switch your speech to the representational system the child accesses in? Did you find some of the effects you got in the listening exercises?
4. Again, did you find the child you got along with better was organized more like you are than the one you don't get along with? Does this give you some more ideas about expanding your flexibility?

Eye movement accessing cues are valuable signals. But they are still only one of many things to watch for and use. The body can give you so many signals that it is almost unbelievable. Besides the eye movements, the next place to look is at breathing. Many people seem almost unable to think and breathe at the same time. It's something like the inability to walk and chew gum, only less funny. It is especially noticeable when people are stuck, confused, or unable to remember something. The trap is that, if you stop breathing, your brain won't care so much about remembering anything except how to stay alive. Try holding your breath for twenty to thirty seconds (out of shape, huh?), and then try to remember the capital of Montana or some equally vital bit of information. Or try and do a math problem in your head while holding your breath. Pretty tricky, eh? How do you spell relief?—B-R-E-A-T-H-E!

Watching Experiment Number 2

Step 1

Go find yet another child having some difficulty in class. If you've run out of kids with difficulties by now, go borrow one. Sit in relative privacy with this child and strike up a conversation about the difficulties he or she has been having. As the child begins to describe his or her experiences, watch his or her chest. Notice the breathing or lack of it. Notice at what points it hesitates or stops altogether, and listen for what the child is talking about at that moment.

Step 2

Teach this child to breathe properly. This may sound strange, but it is a very good idea. A full breath starts by filling up the abdomen, then the chest. Just as the chest becomes completely full, the clavicle, or collarbone, will rise slightly. Then both cavities will empty. The breath should be slow and smooth, without stops or interruptions. Try some yourself and find out if you feel more relieved. If you can't do it, find a yoga class, a Zen master, a Tai Chi instructor, or a hospital. When you have taught this child to breathe properly, and you are both doing so, resume the conversation about his or her difficulties. Continually remind the child to relax and breathe, and watch what happens. Then answer the following questions:

1. Are you more aware of how breathing blocks, as they are called, affect thinking in children or yourself?
2. Is this something you noticed before? Has anyone ever mentioned to you or taught you to breathe properly?
3. Did you notice immediate, or almost immediate, relaxation with the first few good breaths in the child or yourself?
4. Does this awaken or reawaken your awareness of the importance of the body to the mind?
5. Can you imagine how chronically tired or generally uncomfortable you would be if your breathing were constantly shallow or interrupted? Take a look around your classroom.

Eye movements and breathing patterns are the two easiest things to see in another person. They tell you a lot. In addition to those, there are certain kinds of muscle tensions that indicate emotions and discomfort. They aren't perfect indicators, but they aren't bad either. The study of body psychology is advancing all the time. The general public, however, still hasn't gotten much of the message. The following experiment will help you become aware of some of the most common and obvious muscular indicators of discomfort.

Watching Experiment Number 3

The following are common body cues to watch for:

raised or tight shoulders	anger, fear, or both
stiff or tight jaw	anger, fear, or both
wrinkled or strained forehead	anger, disgust, eye strain
slumped shoulders	sadness, fatigue
arms/shoulders held back	fear of contact or fear of "doing"
slumped appearance/chest caved in	hurt (emotional), fear

Even though you are at least intuitively aware of these, consciously watching for them can be quite helpful. There are many more, of course, but these six are enough for now.

Step 1

Familiarize yourself with the above list and any other similar indicators that you think you'd like to experiment with. Since all of these occur in all of our behaviors, choose one at a time to experiment with. Starting with, for example, raised and tightened shoulders, spend three or four days watching for this in your classes. Again, don't stare, just notice. If you stare at anyone, they are liable to hunch their shoulders. Don't cause it, just notice it. Spend three or four days on each of these body cues.

Step 2

When you think you can readily spot the occurrence of any of these, start paying attention to your own behavior. If you notice several children exhibiting the same or similar cues all at the same time, stop what you're doing for a moment. Check your own breathing, posture, and bodily tension. If you are tense, relax. If not, see if there is something going on that might be producing this response from the children. If so, change it. This is called flexibility of behavior.

Step 3

If you have noticed some children consistently responding in rigid patterns with their bodies, congratulations! If not, go back and look again. We all develop ways of holding or tensing our bodies at an early age. This is built into family life. It isn't good or bad, it just is, so start to notice how it affects the kids in your class.

Step 4

Now you have a chance to really help one of your kids to grow. Choose one of the children who is rigidly holding some part of his or her body. Teach that kid to relax the muscles he or she has been holding tensed. Then have him or her alternate between tensing and relaxing those muscles. This is one of those times when a gentle and loving touch is really appropriate. Ask how they feel as they tense or relax their muscles. The above interpretations (for example, anger or fear with tightened jaw muscles) may or may not be correct for this child. It doesn't matter. Find out what is.

Step 5

To really teach this child about his or her body and emotions, do the following: when he or she can relax and tense those chronically-held muscles at will, teach the child to breathe properly. Then experiment with the connection between breathing and tightened muscles. It is important for the child to become aware of them on the inside rather than hearing an explanation from the outside. Then ask the child if he or she has ever noticed that these muscles were tight before. If so, when? Then answer the following questions:

1. Was it easy for you to spot muscle tension in the kids?
2. Did you notice some of the children looking tense all over? Are they the ones who have the most trouble in class?

3. Did you notice that the more tension a child was holding, the worse his or her breathing was?
4. Were you able to help the child learn to feel more comfortable?
5. Can you imagine other, more general ways to teach the children bodily awareness?

The object of these experiments, both listening and watching, is not to drive you crazy trying to sort out visual and auditory input. It's to make you a better teacher. I know there are too many things to consciously watch and listen for. That's why we do these experiments. Practicing them will teach you to be proficient on an unconscious level. You will be able to do it automatically.

For those who say there is just too much to try and sort out, I say ridiculous! People constantly amaze me when they try to tell me all of the things they can't do. Consider a common activity: Driving an automobile. To perform this task, you have to do the following:

1. Watch the road ahead of you.
2. Watch two or three rear view mirrors as well as both sides.
3. Sort out the important or dangerous hazards and obstacles in at least four directions.
4. Read signs and signals.
5. Operate a steering wheel.
6. Operate two or three foot pedals.
7. Operate a variety of other devices and switches with hands and possibly feet—gear shifts, lights, horn, radio, and so forth.
8. Watch and/or listen to a variety of gauges and lights inside the car.
9. Guide this machine to the exact location you wish to go.

In addition to these, many of us can and do listen to the radio, carry on one or more conversations at various levels of complexity, light and smoke a cigarette, and drink a Coke—all at the same time. Not only that, but a lapse in any of the first seven of these could cost us our lives! I wonder if watching a child's eyes and breathing while carrying on a sensible conversation is really that difficult.

Interesting to me is that in medicine we have a process known as biofeedback. It is a clever outgrowth of some strange psychology experiments performed in 1969. Essentially, someone having muscle tension, headaches, heart trouble, or a variety of other stress-related ailments will come to a doctor's office. A technician will paste electrodes to certain muscle groups on the person's body. The ones listed above at the beginning of this exercise are the most typical. Each of these electrodes is then attached to an instrument(s) that looks something like a piece of stereo equipment. It comes equipped with a dial and headphones. One can watch the gauge and/or listen to the tone rise and fall as his or her muscles tense and relax. The machine gives the person visual and/or auditory feedback on his or her biological functions, such as muscle tension, hence the name biofeedback. Practicing on the machine helps people become aware of tension and stress and helps them to relax. In relatively rare cases, the machines can give feedback on such subtle body mechanisms as brain waves and body temperature. Again, I think this is the highest and most clever use of our technology—not to do boring work for us, but actually to make us better people.

What bothers me is something that I think is a greater comment on us as people. Even though tools like biofeedback are clever and effective, why the hell should we need them? Isn't it bizarre that we are so out of touch with our own bodies that we need machines to teach us what we're feeling? I think it is. I also think that a school teacher could be more proficient at biofeedback than any machine. It takes practice, and that's all. We could probably wipe out most stress-related disorders in a generation. We could also significantly advance the level of general health and education in this country.

Anchoring Yourself

I am sure you've found that with some kids these tasks are easy and with some they're hard. You have undoubtedly found some of the tasks require more subtle discrimination skills than others. You may also have noticed that *you* are more capable sometimes than at other times. Sometimes it can be because of the familiarity of a task, which is doubtful in this case. Other times, it can be your state of mind. We all have off days. We also have days, or at least times, when we are really *on*. Wouldn't it be great to be able to have a switch so that you could just turn yourself on when you need to? Remember anchoring? (See pp. 25, 26, 27 to refresh yourself, if necessary.)

There are certainly some states of mind you want to be able to get to in order to do your best as a teacher. The process of anchoring these is simple. You need only decide what states or experiences you want to be able to recreate in yourself.

Anchoring Yourself Experiment #1

Step 1

Sit in a quiet place where you will not be disturbed. Breathe comfortably and relax.

Step 2

Remember a time when you felt you had your class in the palm of your hand, one in which you and the children were enjoying yourselves and learning together effectively, a memory in which the energy level in the room seemed just perfect and everyone was comfortable.

Step 3

Close your eyes. Imagine, for about five minutes, that you are back in that same classroom experience again. You might start by visualizing the door to the classroom. As you imagine walking through the doorway, see the room. Listen to the sounds there. Become aware of the smells and tastes of that room. Pay especially close attention to your feelings. Get as close as you can to the actual feeling sensations you had at that time. You'll know when you get there.

Step 4

When you have the feelings the way you want them, anchor yourself. To do this, touch the tip of your thumb to the tip of your forefinger on your left hand. Use light but noticeable pressure. This is your general resource anchor for the classroom.

Step 5

Stand up, walk around, and take a few more deep breaths. Take a two or three minute break. Have a cookie. (It seems like a nice idea, but it's optional.)

Step 6

Sit down again and repeat steps 3, 4, and 5. It should only take a couple of minutes.

Step 7

Sit down again and "fire" your anchor by touching your thumb and forefinger in exactly the same way. Feel the feelings, then answer the following questions:

1. When you fired the anchor in step 7, did the feelings come back as before? Were they as intense? How about visual images? Sounds? Smells?
2. Wasn't this easy?
3. Are there other areas of your life besides teaching in which you would like to be able to access your internal resources? I sure hope so!!

Anchoring is almost unbelievably powerful. Sometimes, though, it takes a bit of practice. Further, there is no reason it has to be done with touch. I only chose that particular method because it seems an easy way to start. Besides, you have three more fingers and a whole other hand to continue with if you want to. That can give you a total of eight anchors ̣ use at will. Other internal states to anchor include the ̣lowing:

creativity	relaxation	curiosity
motivation	tolerance	humor
courage	patience	
excitement	perseverance	

The list of possibilities is almost limitless.

There are other convenient ways to set up anchors besides touch. Easiest for some people is to remember a particular visual image. An example might be the face of a particular person that produces a special feeling. That is how many people come to idolize someone. The internal image of that person's face is an anchor for a feeling of awe or reverence. Other people find sounds or words to be better anchors for them than either touch or imagery. These people will often have that one special song (as in "they're playing our song") to produce a passionate feeling or memory. How about words that produce a powerful feeling? George Carlin's "the seven words you can't say on television" immediately comes to mind. Actually, all words are just anchors to particular experiences. That's why we have them.

Anchoring Yourself Experiment #2

Step 1

Pick a time or subject in class that has been particularly troublesome or difficult for you. Decide, from the following list, which internal resources would make this difficult task easier and more enjoyable.

creativity	patience
motivation	humor
relaxation	perseverance

Step 2

For each of the above resources you choose, remember a time when you had that resource available: a time when you were extremely creative, motivated, patient, and so forth.

Step 3

Imagine yourself back in that situation, as you did in the last experience. See the room or place as you did then, hear those sounds again, recall those distinct smells and tastes.

Step 4

When the feelings are as close to those original feelings as possible, anchor yourself. You can use a touch. For example, touch the tip of your thumb to the tip of another finger. As an alternative, you may use a word or phrase. If you would like to try a sight-oriented anchor, go ahead. With that method, it may be easiest to look at some unusual object in the room. With practice you may try an internal visual image to anchor yourself with.

Step 5

Stand up, walk around, have a cookie, and so on.

Step 6

Sit down again and repeat steps 3, 4, and 5.

Step 7

Sit down again and fire your anchor. Feel the feelings.

Note: An anchor will either work or it won't. Be willing to try one, two, or three times. If it doesn't seem to work when you fire it, simply try another. That's why we test them.

Step 8

Once you have the effective resources you need at your command, imagine you are in that troublesome classroom situation. See the room, hear the sounds in the room, and so on. When you have the feelings that go with that difficult situation, fire your anchor(s). Hold it for about a minute, then answer the following questions:

1. How was it trying to anchor in different representational systems, that is sound, sight? Easy? Hard?
2. What happened when you imagined yourself in the difficult situation and fired your anchors? Did you feel strange or confused? Don't worry, those feelings are common.
3. When you think about that problem situation now, is it different somehow? Imagine you are in that difficult setting now. Are the feelings different?

This is a simplified version of a standard NLP technique called collapsing anchors. It is a way to (sort of) inject needed internal resources into a situation in which they are lacking. Once the changes happen on the inside, they will usually follow on the outside. This next experiment will help you insure this by adding a step known as future pacing.

Anchoring Yourself Experiment #3

Step 1

I firmly believe that any way you improve as a person will improve you as a teacher as well. Therefore, this time you have the choice of choosing an area of teaching or an area of your personal life that you would like to improve. It doesn't need to be a real problem. Rather, choose some area that you would like to handle better in some way. Perhaps you should choose something that you do adequately, but that you would like to do excellently!

Step 2

Imagine you are in this situation. Experience it as if you are really there. When you get there, anchor it. I know it may seem strange anchoring the limited situation you have chosen, but don't worry, do it anyway. This time, anchor by squeezing your knee with your hand.

Step 3

Stand up, walk around, eat something nonfattening. Go through the process again.

Step 4

Test your anchor by firing it. Remember to squeeze the spot with the same pressure. If the experience immediately comes back, fine. If not, go through the anchoring process some more until it does.

Step 5

Take another walking-around break. Breathe, drink something (whatever you want), and relax.

Step 6

Now decide what internal resources or experiences you would need in order to improve the experience you just anchored.

Step 7

When you have decided, remember a time when you had those resources.

Step 8

Imagine you are there again. When you have the feeling you want, anchor yourself. This time use the other hand, on the other knee.

Step 9

Take a break and repeat the anchoring process.

Step 10

Test this anchor as you did the others. Fire the anchor. Make sure you have this resourceful experience at your command.

Step 11

Now you have two anchors. On one knee, you have anchored a limiting experience of some sort that you want improved. On the other, you have the necessary resources to do the job. Both anchors work to bring out those experiences in you. Fire them *at exactly the same instant.* Hold them for thirty seconds. Then let the limited anchor go. Five seconds later, let the resource anchor go. This process is called collapsing anchors.

Step 12

Next, imagine yourself in the near future. In your mind, go through the next time you will be in that limited experience. It could be Monday morning at school or whatever is the next likely occurrence of it. When you are really there, fire the resource anchor again. This will add "juice" (technical term). This step, as discussed earlier, is called future pacing. Answer the following questions:

1. When you collapsed the anchors, what happened? Strange feelings? Pleasant feelings? New realizations?
2. When you imagine that *next time*, does it look (sound, feel, and so forth) better? Are you looking forward to it?

Anchoring is the most powerful and effective way of mobilizing your resources. It is also quick and easy. If you make it a habit, you'll thank yourself. But anchoring is too good to hoard. The children you teach deserve to have all their resources in class. School is supposed to make them better people also. Let's do it!

Anchoring Others

Many kindergarten teachers use anchoring. They just don't know it by that name. Remember when you were a little kid and your kindergarten teacher wanted the whole class to stop what they were doing and gather around? Did she play a few notes on the piano? Always the same notes, tempo, and volume? Didn't it work really well? It sure did for my kindergarten class when I was five. In fact, with the exception of paint splattering, my kindergarten teacher standing at the piano, patiently waiting is *all* I remember of that whole school year. Wouldn't it be great to have your students remember you as the one who taught them to be comfortable, interested, and productive in school?

Anchoring Others Experiment #1

Step 1

Pick a child who needs help in controlling his or her feelings: a child who is moody, overly active, nervous, frightened, or acts in any way that hinders him or her.

Step 2

Watch and listen to this child enough, so that it is easy for you to distinguish his or her comfortable times from uncomfortable ones. Even the most active kids have moments of relative calm. Be able to clearly tell the difference in this child. This is called calibration.

Step 3

Decide what kind of anchor you want to use: touch, words, etc. Some kids don't like to be touched at times (or at all). Do not be intrusive; you have lots of choices.

Step 4

When you notice the child in the state of mind you think is most appropriate, for example, calm, attentive, interested, comfortable, and so forth, anchor it. The same rules that applied to you apply here. If you are using a touch, and that is often the simplest way, make sure you know exactly where and with how much pressure you touch the child. Also, make it natural. Don't run down the aisle and dive on his or her arm. Just touch the child comfortably when you are already there.

Step 5

Repeat the last step six to eight times. This should be sufficient to establish the anchor.

Step 6

Test the anchor: when the child is in some neutral state, fire the anchor. See what changes occur. Then answer the following questions:

1. How did you feel setting up this anchor? What were your thoughts as you did so?
2. Did you wonder if your perceptions of this child's state of mind were accurate? With this in mind, did you really know what you were anchoring?
3. Did six to eight times seem like too many? Too few?
4. When you tested the anchor in step 6, what happened? Did you notice changes? Were they subtle? Dramatic? Did the child look different? Sound different?

This experiment constitutes the simplest method of anchoring. You simply wait until the person is in the state of mind that is most useful at the time. Then you anchor it. Once anchored, it becomes a tool at your disposal to help this child whenever needed. You should get in the habit of doing this. It will become totally automatic with practice.

Anchoring Others Experiment #2

Step 1

Choose three children to experiment with. Repeat the above experiments. This time, anchor each child in a different representational system, that is, touch, sound, and sight.

Note: anchoring with touch should be easy by now. For the child you are using sound with, pick a word or phrase you don't usually use. Take a few seconds to practice saying it with a particular voice tone. An example might be saying the words, "It's OK, relax," with a low, soft tone. For a visual anchor, choose a hand gesture that is natural, but that you seldom use. Add a particular posture and facial expression. Remember: with all three, it should be out of the ordinary (for you), natural, and identical each time.

Step 2

When you have established the anchors with the children, and tested them in a neutral situation, you will be ready to move on. For each of the children, wait until they are in the state you experience as a problem for them. Then fire the anchor you have established for their resource state and hold it. Wait a few seconds for the changes to appear.

Step 3

When the child has gone to the resource state you anchored, or some reasonable alternative to the one he or she was in before you fired the anchor, future pace. Simply say something to this effect: "Now, the next time you find yourself . . . (problem state) . . . you'll remember that you can . . . (resource state)." If the child was getting frustrated or stuck, and you fired an anchor for calmness, you might say: "From now on, whenever you feel uptight or frustrated, you'll remember the best thing to do is just calm down." As you say, "calm down," fire the anchor again.

Step 4

Sometimes this is enough to produce a real and lasting change in the child's experience and behavior. Often, however, it will take more than just once. Be willing to repeat steps 2 and 3 until you are satisfied that permanent progress

has been made. That is called perseverance. If you need more
of that, anchor it in yourself!

Questions:

1. Which representational system(s) was easiest for you to
   anchor in? In which do you need more practice?
2. Did you find it taking fewer tries to have the anchor
   established?
3. Are you finding your perceptual ability improving?
4. Did you find this method of anchoring and future pacing
   to be as easy and effective as it is?

You may have children that you feel would benefit from
learning to anchor themselves. Really, all children can, provided that you pace and lead them through it effectively. You
can even do it with a group or class. You have the choice of
doing all the work yourself, having the child do all of it, or
some combination. The following experiment will be a good
start for you.

Anchoring Others Experiment #3

Step 1

Choose a child you think could immediately benefit from
learning anchoring. Perhaps you have someone (or a roomful)
who has real problems controlling his or her feelings and
knows it.

Step 2

Find a time when this child seems to be at his or her very
best. He or she is comfortable, relaxed, and attentive. Compli-
ment the student on his or her present behavior and take the
child aside somewhere. It will only take five minutes.

Step 3

Tell the child that you have discovered, or know, a way that
people can feel this way whenever they want. Tell the child

that it is easy and fun. Then ask if he or she would like to learn. With a setup like that, the answer will be yes.

Step 4

Show the child how to anchor with the thumb and forefinger, just as you learned.

Note: Don't get theoretical or fancy in your explanation to the child. He or she doesn't really need to understand Pavlov to make it work. You might say something like the following: "This is like making a light switch for yourself, except with this switch, instead of a light going on, a feeling will." That's really explanation enough.

Step 5

Future pace by saying something like, "From now on, whenever you feel this way at school, home, or wherever, just use your anchor (or light switch) and you'll be able to."

Step 6

Agree on a signal between the two of you: a gesture, word, or whatever. Use the signal to remind him or her to use the anchor when you think it's appropriate. Tell the child it is just a helpful reminder and that you are leaving the decision (responsibility, choice) up to him or her.

Questions:

1. Was the child surprised or intrigued by your offer? Offers like that don't come along every day.
2. Did you find it very simple to teach anchoring to this child?
3. How well did it work? Was it as effective as doing the anchoring yourself?
4. Did this alter or improve your relationship with this child?
5. Did you notice the child using the anchor often? Did it seem to become a usual part of the child's behavior?

6. Were there other related or seemingly unrelated changes in the child? Improved self-confidence perhaps?

It should be apparent to you by now that you have many choices in using anchoring. You can anchor the child yourself or let the child do it. When you do it you have the choice of explaining it to the child, or keeping it to yourself. Also, there are almost limitless ways of establishing the anchor in any of the three primary representational systems. Further, you have the choice of waiting for the child to move into the state of mind you want anchored, or leading the child to that state. An anchor can be saved for a special time or collapsed with another anchor to produce a change. The most effective communicators can anchor entire audiences at once or different things in different members. With all of these possibilities to explore, you should be able to keep busy for a while longer, perfecting your skills. Have fun!

Guided Fantasy

In the last set of experiments, I instructed you to anchor states as they were occurring in the children. Utilizing what a child presents to you is most of what communicating with your students is about, but it isn't all. If we could only use what we already had, we would be extremely limited. But if we were meant to be that limited, we would not have been given an imagination. As long as we have it, we may as well use it to its utmost.

Most of us know that metaphor is one of the most powerful ways to communicate that man has ever devised; probably one of the oldest, as well. But powerful communication between people is much more than just the transfer of information. If that was all there was to it, things would get mighty dull. Besides, we can all transfer information towards another person. But making it meaningful and have impact on that other person is another story.

A good storyteller involves his listener. His voice becomes a symphony. His expressions and movements paint the most vivid of scenes. His words delve down to the deepest levels of feeling, leaving a taste of experience not soon to be forgotten.

All the while, this artisan of words watches the listener, knowing the effects of his words are truly felt. His presence is totally captivating.

The crux of the process is direction or, as a magician might say, misdirection. Remember my little classroom trips earlier in the book (see pp. 30, 31, 32)? These were nothing more than stories we call guided fantasies. They were designed to go in particular directions, however. I would tell the child what to see and hear in his or her mind. Usually the child would be feeling good and comfortable. In that case, I would simply tell him or her to pay attention to those good feelings while seeing and hearing what I had suggested. This would anchor good feelings to the sights and sounds of the classroom. I would also throw in lots of statements, such as, "And from now on, you will have these good feelings whenever. . . ." It is the way the stories are told that makes them effective.

Think about this: imagine playing tennis, football, jogging, and so forth; remember hearing one of your favorite jokes; or pretend you can smell the aroma of your local bakery. You will get back some of those original experiences. You may become excited, start to laugh, or get hungry (hopefully in that order). In fact, the experiments on anchoring yourself were designed to take you through your own guided fantasies and to bring back useful and pleasant experiences from your past.

There are far more choices than just past experiences, though. Again, that is why we have imaginations. You can use any experience from the past or the future and embellish it all you want. You can also borrow or steal an experience from some other person. Still you can add, subtract, or distort it ad infinitum. One of the most fun ways is to make them up entirely. Some people make up extremely expensive, highly technical guided fantasies. They call them funny names like *Star Wars* and *Raiders of the Lost Ark*. If they are clever enough, millions of people will pay their hard-earned dollars to experience these fantasies. Not only that, but they pay to experience them over and over. I remember seeing *Gone With the Wind* about the same time I took American History in high school. I remember more from that movie than I do from studying the same events in class, maybe even the whole year! I'll probably never forget Scarlet O'Hara or Rhett Butler. I'll probably never remember my history teacher. I looked at him or her far more than four hours, though.

Be all that as it may, the point is still that a good teacher will make a meaningful impact on students. He or she does this by involving them in some sort of experience. The following experiments are designed to sharpen your skills at creating meaningful experiences to produce specific results.

Fantasy Experiment #1

Step 1

Your first task is to write a guided fantasy and to use it for relaxation. Standard ones include (1) walking along a beach on a warm day (2) walking through the woods (3) sitting down in a large field of flowers, and so forth. You may choose any of those or your own favorite. Simply pick one.

Step 2

Sit down with a pencil and paper and make lists of the things you would see, hear, feel, taste, and smell in the setting you chose. If you chose the beach, your list would look something like this:

see	hear	feel	taste/smell
clouds, shapes	waves	warmth of	salt air
bright sun	birds	sun	humid odor of
horizon	wind in	hot sand	the sea
sea gulls	trees	breeze	
pale brown sand		across skin	
blue-green water			

Step 3

Now choose a student you think needs to be able to relax more.

Step 4

Take this child to a quiet, comfortable place. Have him or her sit or lie down, relax, breathe comfortably, and close his or her eyes.

Step 5

Start by saying something like, "Now let's imagine, or pretend, we are taking a trip to . . ." Then continue by describing the scene. Have your list ready to remind you. Begin with visual descriptions, then add sounds, then feelings, tastes, and smells. Talk slowly, in a calm, even voice. Describe this scene and the calm, relaxed feelings that go with it for no more than five to seven minutes. When the child appears to be as relaxed as needed, say, "And from now on, whenever you need to be relaxed, like you are now, you can simply remember this little trip."

Step 6

Tell the child: "It is time to come back to the room now, so take a deep breath, slowly open your eyes, and tell me how that was for you."

Step 7

Find out if this was comfortable and enjoyable for this child. Tell him or her that you do this sometimes yourself. Compare notes. Then answer the following questions:

1. Were you surprised at how effective this was?
2. Using your list, was it easy for you to make vivid descriptions?
3. Did you find yourself relaxing, or did this feel like work?
4. Did this seem to alter the way you and this child relate to one another?
5. How long did the relaxed effect last?
6. Would you be willing to do this on some sort of regular basis with this child? Perhaps once or twice a week for three or four weeks?

This technique is becoming popular among special education teachers. I have seen reports of semi-miraculous improvement in classes of "hyperactive" or "combative" children. This guided fantasy technique became a daily routine in some of these classes. The teachers had some extra training and really dedicated themselves to making it work. Apparently, the kids enjoyed this activity to the point that they actually looked forward to their little breaks from standard classroom routine. Also, they learned to cooperate with each other much better.

Fantasy Experiment #2

Step 1

This time pick a child who could use one of the resources we talked about earlier, i.e., motivation, creativity, perseverance, and so forth.

Step 2

Talk with this child about a time when he or she experienced this resource. Ask the child to remember a time when he or she felt this way and to describe it to you.

Note: Depending on the child's state of mind, this may or may not be easy. Take your time and be encouraging in a positive manner. Also, you don't have to find a memory that is *perfect,* just one that will come close to the feelings you want this child to have.

Step 3

Notice the changes in the child during the description of the experience. Then, tell the child you want to pretend that it is happening again.

Step 4

Have the child close his or her eyes and say something like, "Let's go back to that good time, now." Begin to feed back the child's description of that experience. This time, though, add to it. Make sure that you include at least sights, sounds, and feelings in your description. Do this for about five minutes. When you think the child is having the set of feelings you want, say something like, "From now on, whenever you need to feel this way, you will remember_____." Have the _____ be some very specific feature of this experience for the child.

For example, you may want the child to have feelings of excitement. The child might then describe an experience of going to an amusement park. You may describe back to him or her the sights, sounds, and feelings of an amusement park, based on a combination of his or her description and your own experience. At the end of the description, you might say, "And from now on, whenever you want to feel this way, you can just remember that roller coaster."

Step 5

The nice thing about doing it in this way is that the child now has an anchor for that feeling and so do you. In the above example of the roller coaster anchor, the child can remember the roller coaster whenever he or she thinks it is necessary. Or, if you felt at some time that it would be good for the child to have that feeling, you could simply ask, "Remember that roller coaster?" In remembering it, those feelings will come back to the child. Test the anchor to make sure that it works for both of you. Then answer the following questions:

1. Was it easy for the child to remember a useful experience? Did you have to suggest one?
2. From the child's description, were you able to get enough to start with?
3. Was it easy for you to embellish the story? Did you find yourself going through a similar experience to help fill in the blanks?
4. Did both you and the child enjoy this?
5. How well did the verbal anchor work for you?
6. Did you find that your relationship with this child improved?

The interesting thing about this sort of shared experience, between you and the child, is that it will make you more of a person in his or her eyes. Children often forget that teachers are people too. Letting them know of experiences you both have in common, such as roller coaster rides, is a good reminder for them. Another really nice thing is that these are semi-universal experiences. There are some things that just about everyone has seen, heard, and felt. Amusement parks are OK in some places, but more universal are certain TV programs that most kids watch, that first try at riding a bike, that trip to the zoo or museum that most children living in cities have had, and so forth. Most important is that the child has the experience that will be most useful on the *inside*. How he or she gets *to* the internal experience is less important.

The best thing about these somewhat universal experiences is that they allow you to work with a group of children with the same ease as an individual child. You can easily take the class through a fantasy of an amusement park, even if some of the children haven't been to one before. If your description is good enough, they'll get the feelings anyway. You can certainly use the same anchoring technique as in the above exercise with the whole class. It isn't any different than the kindergarten teacher's piano. If you thought about it for a few minutes you could probably think of several universal experiences for your repertoire.

Fantasy Experiment #3

Step 1

Choose a resource you would like your class to experience: curiosity, motivation, excitement, perseverance, enjoyment are all fine. Choose just one, though.

Step 2

Next, think of a situation that would naturally produce this feeling in everyone. Fantasize. The experience needn't be one that you or the children have ever had.

For example: to produce a feeling of curiosity, a trip to the bottom of the ocean in a submarine might be fun. Or perhaps a visit to a strange planet. Remember, it's a fantasy, so make it fun.

Step 3

Make another list of the visual, auditory, and kinesthetic (olfactory and gustatory, if appropriate) components of this experience.

Step 4

From your list, write out, or at least outline, the fantasy so that you are sure it will produce the feelings you want the kids to have.

Step 5

Take the entire class on this trip into fantasy. You can have them close their eyes and relax, to start with. From then on, it is all yours. It should last about ten to fifteen minutes for the best effect. Talk slowly and enjoy it! When you are satisfied that the children are experiencing the feelings you want them to, anchor them as you did in the last exercise.

Step 6

Have a brief discussion with the class afterwards. Get useful feedback. Then answer these questions:

1. Was it easy to think of an experience that would produce the specific feelings you wanted?
2. Did the class enjoy this?
3. Did you enjoy the creative process yourself?
4. Have you learned some useful things that will make you a better storyteller or communicator?
5. Do you have an appreciation of how moviemakers coordinate sight and sound to produce a feeling in an audience? And how difficult it is to produce the same feeling in everyone?

6. Do you think you will be more aware of your presentation of *all* classroom material from these experiments?

For years, teachers have been telling me that they are fed up with lengthy, theoretical discussions that lead nowhere. Constantly, they have asked me and others for how-tos, the real nuts and bolts of teaching and helping kids. Well, with the technology available now, the question is less "how to" and more "how many ways and where shall I start?" That is what this chapter has been about. It is structured to help you learn pacing, leading, anchoring, and future pacing. Your choices within each of these are as varied as your imagination.

NLP is not an abstract theory. It is the study of how things work. Once you know how they work, you have many more choices about making them happen. The techniques in this chapter were not invented. They were discovered, and they were discovered in the behavior of some of the most powerful communicators that have ever lived. NLP is about studying the most effective behavior you can find. But why stop there? Even the best you can find can probably be improved and/or combined with more of the best from somewhere else. It takes a bit of practice, but that's the fun!

We have the technology to solve almost any of the problems any teacher will ever encounter. But problem solving isn't all there is. That same technology can make us all better people as well. The responsibility that comes with technology is to use it wisely, but to use it. There are no valid excuses left for doing a bad job. Anything can be done badly. That just teaches us how to do it better.

I heard someone describing comedian/author/actor/ producer/director Woody Allen on TV. They were talking about his renowned neuroses and lack of self-confidence. The most fascinating thing said was that when Allen is directing an actor, he takes total responsibility for the outcome of the scene. If the actor acts poorly, Allen apologizes for not having explained himself properly. He never complains about the actor, only his own poor direction that made the actor look bad. Then he explains what he wants again, and they do it until it's the best it can be. We should all have that neurosis.

Notes

Chapter 6

1. "Chunk down" is an NLP term for breaking down into smaller chunks.

CHAPTER 7

TO PARENTS

What did you want from your parents when you were in
school? Can you remember? Probably, you wanted something
more, something less, or something different from what you
got. I seldom meet anyone who is totally satisfied with the way
he or she was parented. I suppose some measure of imperfec-
tion is inevitable.

I believe that one of the trickiest parts of parenting is relating to kids about school. Arranging the respective roles of
parents, children, and school involves a number of choices.
Primary is deciding how school fits in, or does not fit in, to
family life. Some parents think of school as an extension of
home. But it really isn't, and kids are seldom able to think of
it in that way.

More apt is the description I once heard from a juvenile-
court judge. He said that children have two jobs in growing up.
One is to play; the other is to go to school. It is an outgrowth
of our play-versus-work ethic in this country. It's a real pity
when we have to separate the two in our minds. Personally,
I refuse to. But most kids seem to think of school as their *job*.

Think about your own job or jobs you have had in the past.
A job can be drudgery, pain, misery, and exhaustion. It can
also be challenging, exciting, and fun. Most often, it will provide bits of all of those. How about the relationships you've
formed at work? Many people think of their boss as a mean

dictator. He or she could also be a caring and supportive gui
or a combination of both. How about co-workers? Can't the
be anything from a tremendous help to a massive hindrance,
from good friends you enjoy to people you want to avoid?

Then there is the question of basic needs and wants. Besides
getting paid, most people want other things from their job.
Some primarily want to learn and to progress. Others want
stimulation and excitement. Most want, and need, a sense of
accomplishment. Others need to bolster or develop their confi-
dence and self-esteem by doing a good job or by doing something new and creative. How many of us, I wonder, actually
get all of our needs met at work? Just as important, how many
really enjoy their work? Many people constantly complain to
me that they hate what they do, but they don't believe they
have a choice. Sounds an awful lot like school to me.

For kids, school can be all of those same things that work
is for us. But kids have fewer choices about creating their
experience. It is usually created for them. Children enter
school, wanting to form good relationships with others. They
want to learn, and they have a tremendously high level of
curiosity. They also want to feel good about themselves, good
about others, and just plain good. The extent to which a child
develops and achieves healthy relationships, new learning,
and good feelings is the extent to which school allows him or
her to do so.

The name of the game is experience. The secret is to allow
children to have experiences that are structured enough to
guide them into useful learning, but unstructured enough to
allow children's natural curiosity and creativity to flourish.
Doing things for, or to, children seldom teaches them anything. Mostly, it makes them feel incapable or inadequate.
What's just as bad is that they will think others feel they are
inadequate. Bad idea!

In no area is this more true than in the area of developing
self-discipline. I know few adults who feel that they can discipline and motivate themselves the way they would like to.
Most do so out of routine and habit. This robs them of a feeling
of accomplishment. Usually what they experience is the bore-

dom that comes from acting like a robot: switch on, switch off. It can come from too much discipline from the *outside*. If all you do is follow orders, why bother to motivate or even think for yourself? And, what kind of self-esteem will you develop by just doing what others tell you to do (think, feel)?

All of these things are true for most of us. Some people are more comfortable with more structure, some with less. Eventually, however, we need to develop our own structure.

Most of us need to have what we perceive is a safe environment to do so. This is equally true for children when they are in school and at home. For most people, home is a safe refuge from the world. It should represent some stability, physically and emotionally. If children have love, respect, and a reasonable amount of freedom at home, they will generally develop a substantial level of self-worth to take to school with them. Hopefully, the school will foster this. Sometimes it won't. If the school doesn't foster these feelings, a particularly harmful pattern can develop. The following is an example of this pattern. A child feels good at home and is doing well. Then some difficulty develops in school. The child's self-esteem suffers a blow. Too often, when the parents hear about trouble in school, they immediately *react*. They punish or criticize the child further: the child's safe refuge isn't so safe anymore. Self-esteem suffers at home as well as at school. The cycle builds on itself, then builds lousy anchors for the child.

Parents fall into this trap for a number of reasons. Many are concerned about school, rightfully so, but tend to jump in too fast, trying to make everything OK. It doesn't have to be OK all the time. If it was, kids wouldn't learn to take care of themselves. Some parents automatically assume that the school must know what it's doing. They forget that the *school* doesn't know anything. It's the staff and teachers that know. And they are quite human. Sometimes they know a whole lot of stuff that just isn't so.

Another kind of parent is the one who takes problems in school personally. So many times I've heard anguished parents bitterly ask, "How could my child do this to me?" It is very seldom that a child is doing a school problem *to* anyone.

There are exceptions, but they are far rarer than the complaints from parents would indicate. A little less paranoia and a little more logic goes a long way.

Understanding schools and teachers really isn't that much different from understanding kids and parents. Teachers have the same needs from their job that people in general have. To start with, though, teachers are very poorly paid. Second, they are poorly educated to perform their functions. Third, they don't get much respect. Everyone knows of the massive problems of education, but few will recognize an individual teacher who does WELL. While the job of a teacher is certainly challenging, the rewards are often quite meager. That's a generalization I *am* willing to make.

As a result, teachers, no matter how well-meaning they are, can fall into several traps. The first is disappointment, discouragement, or both early in their careers. I have seen many first- and second-year teachers in despair over the difference between what they expected and what they have found in their profession. Those who don't or can't make the adjustments they need, stand a real risk of falling into the second trap: burnout. The symptoms include apathy on the job and/or in other areas, poor health, seething anger or massive depression, a jaded attitude towards students, and a host of other noxious symptoms to which we don't want kids exposed. But the teacher can't be blamed any more than the social worker, doctor, nurse, policeman, and so forth. Both of these traps represent teachers' ways of rebelling against being stuck in the system, just as the children do. It's a natural response. It is also the reason we have so many good people leaving the profession.

Teachers as a group are catching on to what is happening to them, but so far most of the approaches are remedial. In other words, "When you realize you have burned out for a while, take these steps to recover." That's a far cry from preventing it in the first place, but, one thing at a time. There are ways that parents can help, or at least avoid aggravating, these situations when they run into them: they all boil down to effective communication skills.

First, recognize the teacher(s) as a human being(s). Second, listen to them, just as you should your children. Don't jump in too quickly. I know lots of parents who have told me that allowing teachers to get stuff off their chests can help troubled situations tremendously. I've personally found this to be true repeatedly. Like everyone else, teachers need someone to spout off to. Let's be a little tolerant and a little sympathetic. It's worth it.

Third, and most important, share your experience of your child with teachers. That doesn't mean your pet theories on child development. If you know something that works or will not work with your child, share it. Give an example of a time that it has worked (or not), and make sure the teacher understands. Like everyone else, teachers are usually willing to take advice or try something new if it makes sense to them. Fourth, if you think of specific instances in which the teacher might be able to try something with your child, tell him or her.

When talking with teachers, remember a couple of things. Teachers, kids, and you have similar needs as people. Both you and the teacher really have the same ultimate goal: your child's successful education. Sometimes that goal gets obscured by systemic problems or human weakness. It's OK, that's why we have each other.

At this point you may be saying to yourself, "Gee, these steps seem like pacing, leading, anchoring, and future pacing, with a common worthwhile framework. But how will this help teachers who are discouraged or burned out?" People get discouraged and/or burned out because they have lost sight of their purpose or because they have lost hope. Their needs are no longer being met. Anything someone, especially someone from outside the system, can do to reverse those tendencies will help immensely. *That* will help your children.

It is also an appropriate use of the communication skills presented in this book. Better (more) and clearer communication between parents and teachers is always helpful. Don't forget that the same holds true for parents and children. There is no reason in the world not to help your children with the techniques you've learned here. There sure are plenty of good reasons to do so, though. We have a lot of new technology. It is our responsibility as intelligent people to use it wisely. That means, use it.

For example, you can easily do some of the experiments in the preceding chapter with your own children. Find out what happens. If you impress yourself or learn something important, tell a teacher, or a school board, if you're brave. This is called being a good consumer. If you had an infection and went to the doctor, you'd expect him to use the best treatment available. You pay him to do his homework and keep up with the latest developments. The same with lawyers, mechanics, and anyone else who delivers a service. Expect it from your educational system, and you're more likely to get it. Let them know that you know what is available to them. Let them know you expect them to use what is there for them. If you don't tell them, they won't know. The squeaky wheel gets the grease. Go get it!

CHAPTER 8

DIRECTIONS

What needs to happen next? One of our next steps in education will be to make a major change in its focus. Rather than teaching kids what to learn, we will first teach them how to learn. This is the kind of revolution in thinking that is necessary for advancement of the art and science of education—now. It parallels the technological advancement being made in a variety of fields, such as computer science and communication theory. With computer programs now available to the general public and school systems, we'd be foolish to wait around bemoaning the problems we face. We'd be wise to face them with our best tools.

This also (fortunately) parallels advances in thinking in the field of medicine. More and more, doctors and the general public are looking towards viable means of prevention rather than just alleviation of illness. Healthy nutrition, exercise, a *lifestyle* of health, and so on are becoming paramount in many people's thinking. Holistic medicine is making slow but sure strides. Health consciousness is becoming an epidemic. I hope it gets everybody.

How about holistic education? We used to call our most well-rounded and capable people "Renaissance" men or women. But now, we're so worried about "the basics" that we often lose sight of just how much a human being is capable of accomplishing. This is progress?

We are far too concerned with specialization. Teachers get all kinds of specialized training. This leads to separatist thinking. What a loss. We should be teaching teachers and children about connections and "synergies" (the ways in which things fit and work together). If we don't, it will be our loss.

We should also be teaching teachers about systems and organizations. Our failure to do so is like teaching a scuba diver all about the bottom of the ocean, but forgetting to provide him with the equipment to breathe under water. It's a painful thing to forget. Too many of our teachers are sinking, when they need to be swimming. We need them to stay afloat.

Teachers ought to be taught that all systems and organizations have at least two goals. First, their stated purpose. The purpose of education is to help develop the minds and bodies of the current generation of children. Its system and organization must deliver that needed service. But all systems and organizations automatically have another need, one that is seldom stated out loud: survival. This goal has become their prime objective, often to the detriment, if not exclusion, of service delivery.

People working in such systems usually complain bitterly or leave the system. Others burn out. Giving up is not the best use of human ingenuity.

People in the system *are* the system. It may appear to have a life of its own, but that is deceptive and can lead to surrender. If you understand the channels, directions, and processes of communication in the system, you can discover some really useful and fascinating things about how it operates. Information is the lifeblood of social systems. Understanding and influencing the flow of that information creates the ability to influence and control the direction of the system as a whole.

I have worked in hospitals, prisons, and social service agencies for years, as well as consulting in schools. Certain things have been true of all of these settings. First, the people at the top, administrators, wardens, and principals, didn't actually run the show. These leaders surrounded themselves with administrative staffs who did direct things. These staffs weren't always official, either. Sometimes they were just trusted allies, quite often a secretary or two, who had been on the job longer than anyone else, knew where everything was kept, and how anything could be done. Those were the people I got to know first.

Second, there always seemed to be someone at the actual service-delivery level who knew the important information. Again, it didn't matter what the title of that person was: guard, orderly, teacher, nurse, or whatever. For example, a friend of mine used to do consulting in mental hospitals. He insisted that it was far more important to talk with the staff members who worked directly with the patients than to talk with the physician in charge. He reasoned that the doctor could tell you lots of historical and theoretical information about the patient. That's OK, but the staff members could tell you things like, "Don't look cross-eyed at that patient in the corner, or he'll bite you." For some reason, my friend always felt that that sort of advice was real good to have.

People, in organizations, who surround themselves with allies fare far better than those who isolate themselves. Peers can really form solid support groups. They are more likely to effect change than isolated individuals. Sometimes, there really is safety in numbers.

What is the best way to apply these principles to education? First, understand how these naturally occurring phenomena are already in operation. For the sake of survival, and the sacrifice of progress, a lot of people have jumped on the back-to-basics bandwagon. The thinking is that education has gotten too big for its britches, with all its special programs, and has gone downhill. This is partly true, but it is not the whole story. Equally relevant is the reason why so many programs have failed: because they were thrown together just to qualify for federal grants or to satisfy special interests. Because a lot of people have developed ineffective, hodge-podge programs in the name of progress hardly means progress should be abandoned. It simply needs a viable form in which to develop.

Sure, education needs to redeem itself. But simplistic approaches will only limit success to a few areas—that isn't likely to impress anyone. In fact, it will probably go unnoticed as do other small successes. People in this country are impressed by the dramatic. They want to see clear, direct results. NLP technology is powerful enough to provide the drama necessary for this process. It has already done so in the field of psychotherapy. Life-long phobias are being cured in minutes. The same with other major problems people go to therapists for. NLP has revolutionized that profession and will do more in the next few years. In business, this same NLP technology is being used in personnel, employee relations, negotiations, advertising, public relations, and more. Major corporations are regularly using some NLP technology and coming back for more. They have something called a ledger that helps them make the decision. The next field will be education.

Teachers can make this happen. They know their training is inadequate, but their dedication isn't. Just about every teacher I've ever met who has been exposed to NLP has been really turned on. Most are hesitant to take on the responsibility of spreading it around. They feel their responsibility begins and ends in the classroom.

Teachers should teach *up* the "ladder" of their system as well as down, to the children. I know teachers who have pushed for particular programs within their school systems and gotten them through. They have, generally, more credibility with the powers that be than outsiders have. School administrators are less threatened by teachers within their schools than by outside experts. They are more impressed by united efforts of teachers and parents, working through the proper channels, than they are by "renegades" from inside, or outside, the system. I like the renegades better, but school administrators don't seem to share my view.

In this book, we have touched on many of the various troubles in education. Families in trouble can cause children to have trouble in school. Poor funding, outmoded approaches, and bad teaching can certainly cause all kinds of problems. Poor health will certainly undo much of the good even the best schools can provide—that includes a poor diet. All of these things are relevant to the overall problems and are important to consider.

This one volume aims at only one major facet: technology. We have what we need—*now*—to be able to teach children exquisitely well. *There are no learning disabilities.* There are only teaching disabilities. They can be alleviated, in most areas quickly and painlessly, by using the new knowledge.

Teachers and parents alike often feel anxious, frustrated, angry, bored, discouraged, and afraid when they run into a problem or group of problems involving school. This can cause confusion. But confusion isn't bad. In fact, it can lead to curiosity. Curiosity can motivate people to look around and to listen for something new and unusual. A curious and motivated person is certainly someone to be reckoned with. These feelings can lead to real creativity and growth. Maybe even a new sense of hope . . .

APPENDIX

APPENDIX I

NOTE: The following is from a friend/student of mine named Judy Kopfler, M.Ed., who is an educational consultant. She was a teacher for nine years in a variety of settings and is quite creative. She found this fantasy in a book. It was written by a prominent neuro-linguistic programmer. She changed and adapted it to her own style, using her creativity. She added her own NLP skills of pacing, leading, anchoring, and future pacing to make a good tool into a great one. Here it is as she presented it to me.

Preface to J.O. Stevens' *Motorcycle Fantasy*—as used by Judy Kopfler, M.Ed.
I have used this guided fantasy with children of all ages in the classroom and with teachers in teacher workshops. Children and adults are amazed at their travels.

From experience, I have found it extremely helpful for children classified as emotionally disturbed or behavior-disordered, learning disabled, hyperactive and with kids who are tense.

The uses are many, and they have all resulted in positive learning. The child/student gains a better understanding, awareness of himself, and is better able to conscientiously control his behavior in an academic and nonacademic environment.

Here are some tips for taking the guided fantasy. Take the trip yourself first, with the help of a friend. After you read the guided fantasy, I will list ways to modify it for children who may not want to go for a motorcycle ride. I find that one idea creates many more and that, with our creative abilities, we can do anything. Relax and pause frequently so that your students have sufficient time to experience this.

Note: Discuss the fantasy only with those who volunteer to do so. Those who don't will learn on their own. Kids love it, and you will see a positive change right before your eyes.

MOTORCYCLE FANTASY

As a teacher and now a teacher/therapist, I would like to thank John O. Stevens[1] for this idea. I have found this can be used with children, teachers, and adults.

To teachers. "Anything you can do to increase communication in your class will reduce your need to impose order by authority. The class will become more a place for listening and learning, and less a place for fighting and antagonism."[2]

Prepare your students for a brief fantasy experience. Speak softly and pause between sentences so they have sufficient time to visualize your instructions. Here goes—

Imagine that you are a motorcycle. Notice what kind you are and what make. You are being ridden now: Notice who your rider is. How do you get along with each other? Have a dialogue with your rider. Finish the dialogue. Become aware of how fast you are going. Where are you? What kind of condition are you in? Notice all of your various parts: is everything working smoothly? Any badly worn parts about to cause trouble? Where are you now? How do you feel as a motorcycle? Your left handlebar has a brake grip for the front wheel; your right handlebar has the acceleration grip. Let the front-wheel brake grip on the left talk with the accelerator on the right. What is each saying and feeling? You are being stopped now. Where did you stop and how? How do you feel after your ride?

After I finish I find it best to ask: who went on the ride? I then ask: who would like to discuss their trip? (Have faith, there will be a volunteer: this fantasy has an amazing effect and it's contagious.) Allow as many as want to discuss their travels to do so. Focus on how they get along with their rider, who their rider is, and how fast they are going. (Please don't overquestion the kids—work only with what they want to volunteer.)

Their description of themselves as bikes and how well they are working will often give you new insights into their unconscious perceptions of themselves. Also, kids who are hyperactive (or, as I prefer to describe them, fast processors of information) travel at one hundred miles per hour or well over that. Anchoring is very effective for students who travel rapidly. I have been able to physically slow down such children by touching their left fist (the brake grip) as I speak to them slowly and softly. I point out that they can set their own speed, slowing down when they are speeding and speeding up when they are tired. Touching the left hand while talking to them is the anchor. I have seen six-year-olds and sixteen-year-olds gain greater control of their behavior merely by squeezing their own left hand. The change occurs within thirty minutes. When they appear to be gearing up, if I pass by them and merely touch their left hand, they immediately begin to slow down.

Note: Taking the ride is of utmost importance. If the student cannot relate to a bike, he or she won't go for the ride. Ask your class, "Who likes motorcycles?" If the response is low, consider using this fantasy in other ways. Try alternative vehicles, such as a ten-speed bike, a jet, a rocket, a car, a go-cart, a horse, even a boat. This fantasy can be modified and molded to fit your specific classroom needs. Use your imagination and your students'.

The following are responses from students and teachers who went for a ride. Kids, at the outset, usually think I'm weird.

I tell them just to humor me and go along: "It's a way of getting out of class without skipping and without a pass!" (That has been rather successful!) Once they become the bike with a rider, they react: smiling or frowning. Some take their best friend, their parents, or me with them. Some go to California, to Florida, to New York. Some travel down country roads, others in the city. Some race in the superdome. One teacher took her most difficult student out on a ride in the country, dropped him off, and headed back to school much to her amazement! (She was shocked, understood her student better, and became much more effective with him.)

All know how fast they are going and what kind of condition they are in. Some kids' bikes are falling apart and end up stopping by crashing into, or through, a wall. I was rather surprised at the kids with that response. I had bought their well-disguised cover of being cool and collected.

Most kids are smiling, calm, and happy when the fantasy ends. They open their eyes and ask to go back to where they were. I encourage them to go back for that ride when they feel discomfort or tension in the classroom or elsewhere. I also ask those who need repairs to their bikes to take care of themselves. To those who crash, I recommend that there are other ways of stopping that wouldn't hurt so much.

The list is endless, the trip is never the same, and the positive changes in your children are more than worth the risk.

Notes

Appendix I

1. John O. Stevens, *Awareness* (Moab, UT: Real People Press, 1971).
2. John O. Stevens, *Awareness* (Moab, UT: Real People Press, 1971).

APPENDIX II

THE META-MODEL
by
Robert Dilts

The meta-model was developed by John Grinder and Richard Bandler to identify classes of natural language patterns as a means to help increase the flow of information between human beings. The basic premise is that words (surface structure) are meaningful only in that they anchor in an individual some sensory representation (deep structure). During the codification of sensory experience into words (as an individual speaks) and the process of decoding (as a second individual listens and transforms the auditory stimulus into his/her own sensory representation) important information can be lost or distorted. Deletions and distortions of experience may also occur within an individual as he/she codes sensory experiences.

The meta-model provides an identification of linguistic patterns which could become problematic in the course of communication and a series of responses through which two individuals may insure more complete communication. Attention to non-verbal gestures and behavior and to context will also greatly enhance the unambiguous transference of information.

I. *Gathering Information*
   A. Deletions
      1. *Simple Deletion:* when some object, person or event (noun phrases or noun arguments) has been left out of the surface structure.
      e.g., I'm really uncomfortable.
      Response: Uncomfortable about what specifically?
      2. *Lack of Referential Index:* when an object or person (noun) that is being referred to is unspecific.
         e.g., a) They never believe me. Response: Who specifically never believes you?
               b) That doesn't matter. Response: What specifically doesn't matter?
      3. *Comparatives Deletion:* when a referent is deleted during a comparison (i.e., good-better-best; more-less; most-least).
      e.g., It's *better* not to force the issue.
      Response: Better for whom? Compared to what?
   B. *Unspecified Verbs:* verbs which are not entirely explicit where sometimes the action needs to be made more specific.
   e.g., He really frustrates me.
   Response: Frustrates you how specifically?
   C. *Nominalizations:* when an ongoing process is represented as a static entity in a way which may distort its meaning.
   e.g., I can't stand her insensitivity.
   Response: Her sensing what about whom? and how specifically?

II. *Limitations to an Individual's Model*
   A. *Presuppositions:* when something is implicitly assumed in the other person's communication which may, if taken for granted, cause limitations to a person's choices about the experience.
   e.g., If you knew how much I suffered, you wouldn't act this way.

There are three presuppositions in this statement: 1) I suffer 2) you act this way and 3) you don't know.

Response: 1) How specifically are you suffering? 2) How specifically am I reacting? 3) How do you know that I don't know?

NOTE: There are a large number of different types of presuppositions that can be identified. For a listing see *The Structure of Magic* by Richard Bandler and John Grinder.

   B. *Modal Operators of Possibility and Necessity:* statements identifying rules about or limits to an individual's behavior (i.e., possibility=can/can't, it's possible/impossible, will/won't, may/may not; necessity= should/shouldn't, must/must not, have to, etc.).

      e.g., 1) possibility: I *can't* relax. Response: What stops you?

         2) necessity: I *shouldn't* let anyone know what I feel about that. Response: What would happen if you did?

   C. *Complex Equivalence:* when two experiences or events come to stand for each other but may not necessarily be synonymous.

      e.g., She's always yelling at me . . . She hates me.

      Response: Does her yelling at you always mean that she hates you? Have you ever yelled at anyone that you didn't hate?

III. *Semantic Ill-Formedness*

   A. *Cause-Effect:* when an individual makes a causal linkage between their experience or response to some outside stimulus that is not necessarily directly connected, or where the connection is not clear.

      e.g., This lecture makes me bored.

      Response: How specifically does it *make* you bored?

   B. *Mind-Reading:* when an individual claims to know what another individual is thinking without having received any specific communication from the second individual.

e.g., Henry never considers my feelings.

Response: How do you know that Henry never considers your feelings?

C. *Lost Performative:* Statements and judgments that an individual considers to be true about the world which may be generalizations based on the individual's own experience. (Lost performatives are characterized by words like: good, bad, crazy, sick, right, wrong, true, false, etc.)

e.g., It's bad to be inconsistent about what you think.

Response: Bad for whom? How do you know that it is bad to be inconsistent?

D. *Universal Quantifiers:* Words which generalize a few experiences to be a whole class of experience (characterized by words like: all, every, always, never, etc.).

e.g., She never listens to me.

Response: She *never* listens to you? How do you know that she *never* listens to you?

APPENDIX III

Behavioral Engineering and the Computer
by
Robert Dilts

Behavioral Engineering designs and produces software for the computer and other interactive media, such as arcade games and video systems, that make *people* more effective and productive. This is accomplished by identifying desired behavioral outcomes and skills and then using the principles and technology of neuro-linguistic programming (NLP) to make an explicit, step-by-step model of the thought processes or mental "programs" that produce that behavior. This mental strategy is then incorporated into an interactive computer or video program, so that when a person plays with or uses the program, the thinking strategy becomes systematically and unconsciously ingrained in the user.

As an educational tool, the computer surpasses other media in that it engages all three of the primary senses simultaneously. School books engage one representational system: visual. Videotapes engage two: visual and auditory. Through its interaction with the user, the computer engages not only visual and auditory, but kinesthetic as well. This accounts for its popularity on the market.

The computer can evaluate the user's response immediately and give the appropriate feedback *while* the user is engaged

146

in the activity of learning. This is something that a book or videotape will never be able to do.

Perhaps the most important feature of the computer is its infinite amount of patience: it gears itself to the pace of the student.

Anyone working with a computer learns a great deal unconsciously while using a program or playing a video game. Programs are designed to utilize and enhance the motivational framework provided by the computer and video environment to help people learn unconsciously and be more productive while enjoying themselves.

For example, the popular Spelling Strategy program (currently being marketed by Apple Computer through their SDS program) leads the user's eye movements and uses color graphics and computer animation to develop visualization. The mental strategy used by almost all successful spellers. The program produces immediate, observable results and has even turned children who were previously thought to be learning disabled into effective spellers.

Programs that install thinking strategies for creative writing, typing, reading, second language acquisition, creativity, and decision making (which innovatively uses the computer keyboard to get unconscious feedback from the user) employ the same principle.

We are committed to integrating the latest computer and video technology with the behavioral technology of neuro-linguistic programming to increase and accelerate human productivity, potential, communication, and evolution on a personal, organizational, and international scale. The Industrial Revolution marked the beginning of man's efforts to develop and refine machines to make them better and more effective. Through these efforts, we now have machines that can help make human beings more effective.

• For further information on specific computer programs contact:

Behavioral Engineering
230 Mount Hermon Rd.
Suite 207
Scotts Valley, Ca. 95066

TEAR-OUT PAGES

Visual accessing cues for a "normally organized" right-handed person.

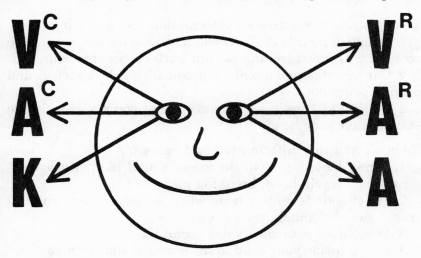

V^C Visual constructed images. V^r Visual remembered (eidetic) images.

(Eyes defocused and unmoving also indicates visual accessing.)

A^C Auditory constructed sounds or words. A^r Auditory remembered sounds or words.

K Kinesthetic feelings (also smell and taste). A Auditory sounds or words.

Tear out page 1

Questions (Note: Forget about the answers, watch the eye movements.)

To elicit visual remembered information and accessing (V^R):
1. What color is your favorite toy (dog, cat, car, hot-air balloon, etc.)?
2. What does your favorite TV star look like? (Small and green?)
3. How many knobs does your TV set (Pac Man, computer, stove, etc.) have?
4. Make a picture in your head of your living room (clubhouse, girlfriend, etc.).

To elicit visual-constructed information and accessing (V^C):

1. What would it look like if you had a purple ice cream cone covered with mustard and peanut butter? (Scrumptious, eh?)

2. Can you imagine a pink elephant with yellow stripes and orange polka dots?

3. Make a picture in your head of what you would look like standing on your head.

To elicit auditory information and accessing (A):

1. What does your favorite record sound like? Musical instrument, bicycle horn, breaking glass?

2. What sounds do you hear when someone plays an electronic game? (Pinball, tennis, etc.)

3. What does your own voice sound like to you?

4. Listen inside your head to the sound of your own voice (or anyone else's; preferably someone who does not evoke an emotional reaction.)

To elicit kinesthetic information and accessing (K):

1. How do you feel right after a big meal? Athletic event, long walk?

2. Do you remember how you felt inside the last time you were really excited? Cold, warm, happy, scared?

3. What does it feel like when you touch something rough, like sandpaper? Smooth like glass, gooey like melted chocolate?

4. Pay attention to how you feel inside your body right now.

Questions that are unspecified regarding sensory functioning:

1. What are you thinking about?

2. How do you know when you are learning something?

3. How do you know when you believe something?

4. What are you aware of?

SPELLING STRATEGY [1]

1. Prepare a list of words or use spelling words from the child's current text.

2. Using the eye-movement-pattern tear-out page, or the skills you have developed in determining accessing cues, find the direction of the child's gaze while he or she is accessing visual-remembered material.

3. Explain to the child that it is easiest to remember what something looks like when his or her eyes are pointed in that direction.

4. Ask the child for his or her favorite color. Explain that it will be more fun to learn to spell if he or she remembers the words in that color.

5. Show the child the first word in the list. Have the child pretend to take a snapshot in his/her mind's eye.

6. Have the child look up and to the left, or wherever you have determined is the best direction, and *see* that picture of the word in his/her favorite color.

7. Ask the child, while s/he looks at that picture, to read the letters to you *backwards*.

Note: Spelling the word backwards insures a purely visual strategy, since it is virtually impossible to sound out a word backwards. For this reason, you may find that children and adults find it easier to spell backwards than forwards.

8. When the child spells the word correctly backwards, ask him or her to spell it forwards.

Note: Errors will occur. Go slowly enough to insure that the child has enough time to get the picture and reproduce it in the proper color. If you notice glances in other directions, usually down and to the child's left, be aware

[1]Adapted from SPELLING STRATEGY by Robert Dilts.

that the strategy is being contaminated. If this happens, gently interrupt the child. You only want the child to go through the proper strategy.

9. Future pace by telling the child, "from now on, whenever you want to spell this word, you will simply remember this picture in your head and spell the word correctly."

10. For each word in the list, repeat steps 5 through 9.

Here are a few tips that will enhance the speed, ease, and effectiveness of the spelling strategy. First, make sure that the child is comfortable at all times. Watch for muscle tension, breath holding, slumped posture, or fatigue. This is not a race. If the child gets tired, stop. If his or her muscles get tense, help the child relax. If necessary remind him or her to breathe.

Take as much time as necessary to explain each step. The child needn't understand the underlying neurological principles involved, just what to do. If he or she does not understand the strategy, your explanation must have been faulty.

Break longer words down into three-letter chunks. This seems to be the chunk size that is easiest to handle. An alternative is to isolate a part of the word that is particularly troublesome for *this* child. For example, "relieve" sometimes causes difficulty because of the *i* and *e* that people often reverse. You may want to isolate *iev* from the rest of the word if it helps. You may need to experiment with each word for each child. With a little practice they'll do the rest.

Some people visualize better than others. If a child has difficulty making an internal picture, there are many things you can do. Ask him or her to imagine turning up the brightness of the picture (just like on a TV set). Find a comfortable level of brightness for the child. Then do the same with the distance of the internal picture. Have the child move it closer and further until it is comfortable and easy to see. Repeat this with the size, clarity, and even the color. Only the child can know what is best. Take the time now. It will pay off later.

Remind the child that with a little practice, this will become automatic. It is easier than riding a bike, tying shoes, or playing games or sports. It is also exactly what good spellers almost always do.

MATH STRATEGY[1]

Note: This strategy is essentially the same as the spelling strategy. All of the tips to enhance the spelling strategy apply here as well. This strategy is for visual memorization. It is ideal for multiplication tables. Using this format, many children have been able to memorize tables through tens or higher in as little as two days. It is also effective for formulas, constants, and anything else the child should have memorized.

1. Prepare a list of formulas or problems you wish the child to know. You can use the child's current text as a source.

2. Using the eye-movement-pattern tear-out page, or the skills you have developed in determining accessing cues, find the direction of the child's gaze while he or she is accessing visually remembered information.

3. Explain to the child that it is easiest to remember what something looks like when his or her eyes are pointed in that direction.

4. Ask the child for his or her favorite color. Explain that it will be more fun to learn math if he or she learns equations in that color.

5. Show the child the first formula or equation (e.g., $4 \times 5 = 20$, $20 \div 5 = 4$, $2 + 16 = 18$, $18 - 16 = 2$, and so forth). Have the child pretend to take a snapshot in his or her mind's eye.

6. Have the child look in the direction you determined in step 3 and *see* that picture of the equation in his or her favorite color.

7. Ask the child, while he or she looks at the picture, to read the equation *backwards*.

8. After the child reads the equation backwards, ask him or her to do so forwards.

9. Future pace by telling the child, "From now on, whenever you want to remember that equation, you will simply remember this picture in your head and remember it correctly."

10. For each equation or formula, repeat steps 5 through 9.

---

[1]Adapted from MATH STRATEGY by Robert Dilts.

MOTORCYCLE FANTASY*

Teacher: Emphasize the italicized words—they are anchors that will be useful from now on. As was discussed in Appendix I, the left hand will be the anchor for slowing down, and the right hand the anchor for speeding up. Where you see . . . pause and allow the children to do or experience what you have just said. Speak slowly and clearly. Once you have done this fantasy, you can repeat it and embellish it as much as you like. The point is the anchors.

Imagine that you are a motorcycle. Notice what kind you are and what make. You are being ridden now. Notice who your rider is . . . How do you get along with each other? . . . Have a dialogue with your rider. . . . Finish the dialogue and become aware of how fast you are going. . . . Notice where you are. . . . What kind of condition are you, the motorcycle, in? Notice all of your various parts. Is everything working smoothly? Any badly worn parts about to cause trouble? . . . Where are you now? . . . Notice how you feel being a motorcycle. Your *left hand*lebar has a *brake grip* for the front wheel . . . and your *right hand*lebar has the *acceleration grip* . . . . Carry on a dialogue or conversation between the front wheel *brake grip on the left* and the *accelerator on the right* . . . . Notice carefully what each is saying and feeling. . . . You are being stopped now. Where did you stop and how? How do you feel after your ride?

---

*John O. Stevens, *Awareness* (Moab, Utah: Real People Press, 1971). It is reprinted, with slight changes, with permission of the author and publisher.

157

COMPUTER FANTASY

Teacher: Emphasize the italicized words. They are anchors that will be useful from now on. When you see . . . pause and give the children time to experience what you have just presented to them. Speak slowly and clearly. This fantasy can be done in the classroom or, preferably, outside—depending on your surroundings. Following the fantasy, have a class discussion about when up time and down time would be useful in class or elsewhere. This fantasy can be repeated and embellished as much as you like. The point, again, is the anchors. Begin with the children standing up.

Pretend you are a very special computer. You are on wheels so that you can move around. This computer takes in data from the outside world through sight, sound, touch, taste, and smell. When it's taking in *outside* information it is in *up-time*.

This computer also processes data on the inside. It makes pictures, hears sounds, talks to itself, has feelings, tastes, and smells inside. It remembers everything. When it is doing these things *on the inside* it is in *down-time*.

Begin by going into up-time. Walk around and take in data from the outside. Look around. What do you see? . . . Now, listen. What do you hear? . . . Touch a few different things. How do they feel? . . . Do you smell or taste anything? . . .

Stop where you are. Close your eyes and go into down-time. Pay attention to the inside. What pictures do you see inside? . . . What do you hear inside? . . . Are you saying anything to yourself silently on the inside? . . . How about smells or tastes? . . .

Spend another minute in *down-time,* aware only of the *inside.* . . .

Now open your eyes, go back into *up-time,* and walk around a bit more. Be aware of what is around you on the *outside.* . . . Stop. Close your eyes again and go back *inside to down-time.* . . . What is happening *on the inside* now? . . . From now on, when I say *down-time,* you'll know to go *inside* . . .

159

Now open your eyes and come back into *up-time*. From now on, when I say *up-time*, you'll know to *pay attention to the outside*.

How was it being a computer? Fun?

SAFARI FANTASY

Teacher: Emphasize the italicized words. Each one specifies sensory functioning. When you see . . . pause and give the children time to experience what you have presented. Speak slowly and clearly. The point of this fantasy is for children to comfortably move from experiencing one sensory mode to another. Following the fantasy, discuss the importance of using all of the senses to fully experience, enjoy, and learn from an event.

Close your eyes. Sit back, relax, and take a deep breath. Let's pretend we are going on a safari through the African jungle. We start at the edge of the jungle where we *see* a path into the trees . . . We're walking in now, *looking* down the path, *feeling* the soft brush under our feet . . . We can *see* lots of strange plant life, animals, shapes, and colors. . . . As we *look* around, we begin to notice the special *sounds* of the jungle . . . We hear the screeches of monkeys in the trees above our heads, the roar of a lion in the distance, the buzzing of insects, . . . and more sounds that we don't understand . . . While we *hear* these unusual *noises,* we notice the *warmth* of the jungle air . . . and we can *feel* the dampness. It makes us feel *hot* and *heavy* . . .

All of a sudden, we *hear* something in the distance. . . . It almost *sounds* like *thunder,* but it doesn't stop . . . We begin to *walk* faster through the *dense* brush toward the *echoing sound* . . . As we get closer, we *hear* water *rushing.* We realize the *sound* we *hear* is a giant waterfall. We become even more *excited* and *anxious* as we *hurry* on our way. . . . We *hear* ourselves *trampling* through the brush. Then we *break* through the trees into a large *clear*ing, and we *see* it: It's the *biggest* waterfall we have ever *seen* . . .

We gather in the clearing to just *sit* down, *rest, watch,* and *listen* to this spectacular sight . . . We think to ourselves how lucky we are to have *eyes, ears,* and *feelings* to *appreciate* the *beauty* around us . . . and we can remember to use all of our senses—sight, sound, touch, taste, and smell—to enjoy and learn as time goes on. . . . Now slowly come back into the classroom. . . .

Did you enjoy your safari? Let's talk about it.

The following is a list of common and useful verbs categorized into representational systems. They will be helpful when you are listening to children's speech to determine which system(s) they are consciously representing their experiences in. They will also help you to switch to representational systems you don't normally use. The list of unspecified verbs will help you become more aware of choices that *don't* lead children into any particular representational system. Feel free to add to this list.

VISUAL	AUDITORY	KINES-THETIC	UNSPECI-FIED
see	listen	bite	seem
view	hear	burst	be
observe	overhear	bend	aware
witness	sound	bind	have
sight	quiet	break	think
spot	order	fall	believe
look	ask	catch	allow
glimpse	beg	fight	become
glance	ring	go	be able
peer	chime	grasp	have to
peek	yell	grab	must
peep	scream	hold	want
survey	sing	hit	shall
eye	speak	climb	know
examine	talk	run	do
inspect	shout	struggle	make
gaze	whisper	throw	understand
stare	groan	walk	create
glare	moan	jump	contemplate
pale	whine	push	ponder
find	buzz	feel	desire
read	call	grip	appreciate
show	click	handle	sense

BIBLIOGRAPHY

Bach, Richard. *Illusions: The Adventures of a Reluctant Messiah.* New York: Delacorte Press/Eleanore Friede, 1977.

Bandler, Richard and John Grinder. *Frogs into Princes.* Moab, UT: Real People Press, 1979.

Bateson, Gregory. *Mind and Nature: A Necessary Unity.* New York: E.P. Dutton, 1979.

Dilts, Robert B., et al. *Neuro-Linguistic Programming I.* Cupertino: Meta Publications, 1979.

Dilts, Robert B. "Math Strategy." A Behavioral Engineering computer program, 1981.

Dilts, Robert B. "Spelling Strategy." A Behavioral Engineering computer program, 1981.

Goodman, Paul. *Growing Up Absurd.* New York: Vintage Books, a division of Random House, 1956.

Laing, R.D. *The Politics of Experience & The Bird of Paradise.* London: Penguin Books, 1967.

Morris, Desmond. *The Human Zoo.* New York: McGraw-Hill Book Co., 1969.

Stevens, John O. *Awareness.* Moab: UT: Real People Press, 1971.

BOOK LIST
Meta Publications Inc
P.O. Box 565   (415) 965-0954
Cupertino, CA. 95015

Thinking About Thinking . . . . $ 9.95
Joseph Yeager (paper)

The Master Moves $14.95
Moshe Feldenkrais

Magic in Action $14.95
Richard Bandler

Roots of Neuro-Linguistic Programming $22.00
Robert Dilts (hardcover)

Applications of Neuro-Linguistic Programming $22.00
Robert Dilts (hardcover)

Meta-Cation: Prescriptions for Some Ailing Educational Processes . . $12.00
Sid Jacobson (hardcover)

Meta-Cation: Volume II $12.00
Sid Jacobson (hardcover)

Phoenix—Therapeutic Patterns of Milton H. Erickson $14.00
D. Gordon & M. Myers-Anderson (hardcover)

Neuro-Linguistic Programming $24.00
Dilts, Grinder, Bandler et al Limited Edition (hardcover)

The Elusive Obvious $20.00
Moshe Feldenkrais (deluxe edition)

Patterns of Hypnotic Techniques of Milton H. Erickson, M.D. . . . . . $ 9.95
Bandler and Grinder
Volume I (paper only)

Patterns of Hypnotic Techniques of Milton H. Erickson, M.D. $17.95
Bandler, DeLozier, Grinder
Volume II (hardcover)

Provocative Therapy $12.00
Farrelly & Brandsma (hardcover)

Gestalt Therapy and Beyond . . . . $ 9.95
Marcus (hardcover)

Changing With Families . . . . $ 9.95
Bandler, Grinder and Satir (hardcover)

The Structure of Magic, Volume 1 . . . . $ 9.95
Bandler and Grinder (paper)

The Structure of Magic, Volume II . . . . $ 9.95
Bandler and Grinder (paper)

Practical Magic $12.00
Stephen R. Lankton (hardcover)

Therapeutic Metaphors $12.00
David Gordon (hardcover)